Resounding Praise for the Work of Roger Dawson:

"I can't believe it! Here's a book that is packed with wisdom that will help anyone improve their life and yet it is easy and fun to read! Amazing!"

—Og Mandino, author of *The Greatest Salesman in the World*

"A fast, entertaining read that should be required reading for anyone who deals with people. Highly recommended."

—Ken Blanchard, coauthor of *The One Minute Manager*

"Roger Dawson's great book will help you create and expand one of the most critical skills to life-long success."

—Anthony Robbins, author of *Awaken the Giant Within*

"I wish I knew what Roger knows about negotiating before I bought my first property."

—Robert G. Allen

# POWER
# NEGOTIATING

*for*

# SALES
# PEOPLE

Inside Secrets from a
Master Negotiator

# ROGER DAWSON

CAREER
PRESS

This edition first published in 2019 by Career Press,
an imprint of Red Wheel/Weiser, LLC
With offices at:
65 Parker Street, Suite 7
Newburyport, MA 01950
*www.redwheelweiser.com*
*www.careerpress.com*

ISBN: 978-1-63265-148-8
Library of Congress Cataloging-in-Publication Data
available upon request.

Cover design by Kathryn Sky-Peck


Printed in Canada
MAR
10  9  8  7  6  5  4  3  2  1

## Dedicated to:

The salespeople of America.

The person at the drive-in window
who asks me if I want fries with that.

The waiter who suggests a better wine.

The retail clerk who cares enough to sell me up
to the top of the line.

The unknown salesperson on the last plane home
on a Friday night, knowing that he or she will be
back at the airport again on Sunday afternoon.

The Wall Street wizard who sells the bonds that
build the cities of this great country.

To every one of you.

You make this country great.

You are the finest salespeople in the world.

If you have any comments, suggestions, stories to share,
complaints to register, or questions to ask, please e-mail the author at:
RogDawson@aol.com

# Contents

# Nothing Happens Until Somebody Sells Something— *at a Profit!*

A lot has changed in the world of selling since I wrote the first edition of this book in 2001.

Buyers are much better informed than they were in the old days. Back then, a salesperson could bluff a buyer by saying, "If you add this to your product line you can expect to see a 20 percent increase in sales." Try that and the buyer will likely punch out a few numbers in his laptop and say, "That's not what we found when we ran a test in our Omaha store. We only got a 4.2 percent increase in sales. Not enough to justify adding another SKU. We did 1 percent better in Chicago, but still not enough to pay off for us."

Retail buyers know exactly what it costs to commit an end cap on a holiday weekend. Or what a free sample clerk will add to a holiday weekend store sales.

Selling is changing in America. It's tougher out there. Competition is sharper than it has ever been. International competition is pushing us to do even better. The competitive advantage of being the first to get a product to market is shortening, from years, to months, to weeks in some industries. Buyers are better negotiators than they used to be. Buyers are better informed than they have ever been.

The buyers to whom you and your salespeople sell have enormous pressure on them to squeeze your prices down even more. Unless your salespeople know how to negotiate well, you can lose profitability, even if sales volume continues to climb. Price pressure has become so great that salespeople who sell to big box stores like Loews and Home Depot dread the line item reviews that happen as quickly as every six months or as long as three years apart. There is a lesson to be learned here that applies to all sales: although the buyer may place a greater emphasis, there are a host of other factors that may be just as important, such as advertising subsidies, guaranteed sales packaging, product labeling, and a dozen more factors.

But one thing has never and will never change: the salesperson gains valuable influence over a buyer when he or she teaches the buyer to do a better job.

Roger Dawson
La Habra Heights, California

# Section One

# The Importance of Negotiating

# Chapter 1

# Selling in the New Millennium

Several years ago I recorded a tape cassette program called *Secrets of Power Negotiating*. To my delight and surprise, it became one of the best selling tape programs of all time. Because of that, sales managers across the country started calling me to come to their company and teach their salespeople how to use Power Sales Negotiating to raise their profit margins and close the sale even against lower-priced competition.

From the giants such as IBM, Xerox, Procter and Gamble, Merck Pharmaceuticals, Abbott Drugs, and General Foods to the smallest entrepreneurial startup companies, I've had a great time teaching, but what is more important, I've learned a great deal about salespeople, buyers, and the ongoing challenge of making the sale. In those years, salespeople have taught me volumes about the selling profession. They tell me that it's getting tougher out there. That only the best and brightest salespeople will grow and prosper in the 21st century. I think that the profession of selling is going to change a lot in the new millennium. Following are some of the challenges I see.

## Trend 1: Buyers are becoming better negotiators

Every salesperson and sales manager whom I meet in my seminars tells me the same thing: Buyers are better negotiators than they were 10 or 20 years ago. That trend is going to continue.

I hate to put this bluntly, but here's what I think has happened. I think that the companies to whom you sell have figured out that the best and quickest way for them to put money on their bottom-line is to take it right off yours!

---

Think about it for a moment. Your customers have three ways to improve their profits:

1. The first way is to sell more. This means either going head to head with a competitor (to improve their market share by taking away some of their competitor's business), or creating new or different products and carving out a new market (something that is very risky and expensive to do).

2. The second way is for them to reduce their operating expenses. This is done by firing employees or buying expensive new equipment.

3. The third way is to do a better job negotiating with you and their other suppliers. This is far easier and it takes money right off your bottom-line and puts it directly onto theirs.

So, what's happening is that companies are upgrading the position of buyer. Whereas 10 years ago you may have been selling to a buyer who moved up through the ranks, now you're dealing with someone who may have a master's degree in business.

He or she may have just come back from a week-long negotiating course at Harvard University. These people know that doing a better job negotiating with you is a much easier way to improve their profits than increasing their market share or trying to shave more off their operating costs.

## Trend 2: Your buyers are better informed than ever

Buyers used to need salespeople because they brought valuable information to the buyer. In the old days, the buyer first learned about new products and new trends in the industry from his regular visits with the salespeople who called on him. That knowledge was power and the salesperson could use it to his or her advantage. That advantage is gone. Buyers get their industry news by programming their computer to bring them news releases on topics that interest them.

In the old days, salespeople could get away with bluffing the buyer. For example, a salesperson who sold to a department store chain could say to the buyer, "If you carry the entire line of SKUs, you'll find that 32 percent of your sales will be in the top-of-the-line model, and your profit margin will go up three points." Nowadays if salespeople try that, they will likely have egg on their face because the buyer will turn to the computer and punch in a few numbers. "That hasn't been our experience," he will tell the salesperson. "We tested that in our Capitol City Mall store and found that only 12.8 percent of our sales came from the top of the line, and our profit margin only went up .8 percent. That didn't even offset our increased cost of carrying the extra merchandise."

Another problem with better informed buyers is that they know if you're offering a better deal to someone else. (It's called "diverting" in the food manufacturing industry.) Let's say that a cookie manufacturer wants to increase the share of market in the Denver area. The manufacturer offers special deals to the stores in Denver to encourage them to load up and promote this brand of cookie. Soon food stores and food wholesalers all over the country are ordering their cookies from Denver instead of from their local distributor to take advantage of the special deal. They don't even have to take delivery in Denver—they simply divert the shipment to their warehouse.

## Trend 3: Salesperson role reversal

It used to be that a salesperson's role was highly defined—to sell the products of a manufacturer to the user or distributor. Now more and more salespeople find themselves going through a role reversal. They have become buyers rather than salespeople. This is very prevalent in industries that sell to retailers, but I believe that it will spread to other industries. Large food manufacturers, such as Procter and Gamble and General Foods, have hired me for just this reason. They want me to train their salespeople how to negotiate cooperative advertising programs with their retailers.

Let's take a salad dressing manufacturer. This may have been an entrepreneur who started out making salad dressing for his own table. His dinner guests enjoyed it so much that he started making small batches for his friends. Then he started mixing up big batches of it for Christmas and birthday gifts. Everyone liked it so much that they encouraged him to put it on the market. So, he takes the plunge. He takes out a small business loan and starts making the rounds of supermarkets and food stores to sell his product to them. To his dismay, he finds that it is very expensive to get his product on a store's shelves. First, he has to negotiate a slotting allowance. "My shelf space is valuable," the store buyer tells him. "If you want us to carry your salad dressing, you must pay us a $20,000 slotting allowance." He may also find that if his salad dressing doesn't sell, he not only has to repurchase the inventory, he also has to pay the retailer a "failure allowance" to compensate the store for the loss of the productive use of the shelf space. When he wants the store to run a special display of his merchandise, he finds that he has to negotiate a payment for a special feature. He also finds that he constantly has to negotiate contributions to subsidize the advertising of his dressings in newspaper ads and flyers that the store mails out. He is spending more of his negotiating efforts buying the store's programs than he is selling his salad dressings.

This is a very typical role reversal for anyone selling to retailers, such as supermarkets, department stores, and specialty stores.

So, the role of the salesperson will change dramatically in the new millennium. Successful salespeople will be more intelligent, more versatile, and better trained than ever. Above all, he or she must be a better sales negotiator.

# Chapter 2

# Win-Win Sales Negotiating

As a salesperson, you've probably heard that the aim of a negotiation is to create a win-win solution. A creative way that both you and the buyer walk away from the negotiating table feeling that you won. You may have had this demonstrated to you with the illustration of two people, both of whom want an orange, but are frustrated because they only have one orange between them. So, they talk about it for a while and decide that the best they can do is split the orange down the middle and each settle for half of what they really need. To be sure that it's fair, they decide that one will cut and the other will choose. However, as they talk about their underlying needs in the negotiation, they find that one wants the orange to make juice and the other needs it for the rind because he wants to bake a cake. They have magically found a way that both of them can win, and neither has to lose.

Oh, sure!

That could happen in the real world, but it doesn't happen enough to make it worthwhile. Let's face it, when you're sitting down in front of a buyer—if you're lucky enough and skillful enough to get to sit down with the buyer—he wants the same thing that you want. There's not going to be a magical win-win solution. He wants the lowest price and you want the highest price. He wants to take money off your bottom-line and put it right on to his.

Power Sales Negotiating takes a different position. Power Sales Negotiating teaches you how to win at the negotiating table, but leave the buyer thinking that he or she won. In fact, the skill to do this defines a Power Sales Negotiator. Two salespeople might go out to meet with two buyers who are in exactly the same circumstance. Both of the salespeople might close the sale at exactly the same price and terms, but the Power Sales Negotiator will leave the buyer feeling that he or she has won. The poor negotiator leaves the buyer feeling that he or she has lost.

> ***Power Sales Negotiators*** **leave buyers feeling that they have won.**
> ***Poor negotiators*** **leave buyers feeling that they have lost.**

I'll teach you how to do this and do it in such a way that your buyers permanently feel that they won. They won't wake up the next morning thinking, "Now I know what that salesperson did to me. Wait until I see him again." No! They'll be thinking what a great time they had negotiating with you and how they can't wait to see you again.

If you'll learn and apply the secrets of Power Sales Negotiation that I'll teach you in this program, you'll never again feel that you lost to a buyer. You'll always come away from the negotiating table knowing that you won and knowing that you have improved your relationship with the buyer.

## Chapter 3

# Negotiating Is Played by a Set of Rules

You play Power Sales Negotiating by a set of rules, just like the game of chess. The big difference between negotiating and chess is that, with negotiating, the other side doesn't have to know the rules. The other side will respond predictably to the moves that you make. From tens of thousands of responses over the years, we know how the other side will react. Not every time, of course, but enough of the time to make negotiating more of a science than an art.

Let me illustrate this point with a little exercise:

Think of a number between 1 and 10.

Multiply that number by 9.

Add the two digits together.

Take away 5.

Translate that into a letter of the alphabet—A, B, C, D, E, F, etc.

Now think of a country that starts with that letter.

Take the second letter of that country and think of an animal that starts with that letter.

Now tell me something: How do I know that you're thinking of an elephant in Denmark?

How do I know that if you live in the Northwest, from Oregon to the Dakotas, you're thinking of an elk in Denmark?

And how do I know that if you're distracted, you got lost on the math and are nowhere close! It's not because I'm a genius. It's because I've done this with thousands of people and I know how predictable the responses are. It's the same way with negotiating. The other side will respond predictably to the moves that you make.

If you play chess you know that players call the strategic moves of the game Gambits (a word that also suggests an element of risk). There are **Beginning Gambits** to get the game started in your direction. There are **Middle Gambits** to keep the game moving in your direction. And there are **Ending Gambits** to use when you get ready to checkmate the other person, or in sales parlance, close the sale.

In the first 22 chapters of this book, I'll teach you the Gambits of Power Sales Negotiating.

First, you'll learn the **Beginning Gambits**, the things that you do in the early stages of your contact with the buyer to be sure that you're setting the stage for a successful conclusion.

This is critical because as the negotiation progresses you'll find that every advance will be dependent on the atmosphere that you create in the early stages. The demands that you make and the attitude you present must be part of a carefully laid plan that encompasses all elements of the negotiation. Your Opening Gambits, based on a careful evaluation of the buyer, the market, and the buyer's company, will win or lose the game for you.

Then I'll teach you the **Middle Gambits** that keep the momentum going in your direction. During this phase, different things come into play. The moves made by each side create currents that swirl around the participants pushing them in different directions. You'll learn how to respond to these pressures and continue to master the game.

Finally, I'll teach you the **Ending Gambits** so you can close the sale after getting what you want while the buyer feels that he or she has won. The last few moments can make all the difference. Just as in a horse race, there's only one point in the contest that counts and that's the finish line. As a Power Sales Negotiator, you'll learn how to smoothly control the process right down to the wire.

# Section Two

# Beginning Sales Negotiating Gambits

# Chapter 4

# Ask for More Than You Expect to Get

Let's start learning the Beginning Sales Negotiating Gambits.

Rule number one is: **Ask the buyer for more than you expect to get.** Henry Kissinger went so far as to say, "Effectiveness at the conference table depends upon overstating one's demands." Isn't that interesting? One of the world's great international negotiators openly says that if you're planning to negotiate with him, you should expect him to ask for more than he thinks he'll get from you. Remember that if you were thinking, "My buyers are not stupid. They'll know the minute I ask for more than I expect to get." Even if that were so, it's still an excellent negotiating principle.

Think of some reasons why you should ask for more than you expect to get.

➤ Why, if you're convinced that the buyer wants to spread the business around, should you still ask for it all?

➤ Why should you ask for full list price, even if you know it's higher than the buyer is paying now?

➤ Why should you ask buyers to invest in the top of the line even when you're convinced they're so budget conscious that they'll never spend that much?

➤ Why should you assume that they will want to buy your extended service warranty, even though you know they've never done that in the past?

If you thought about this, you probably came up with a couple of good reasons to ask for more than you expect to get.

**The obvious reason is that it gives you some negotiating room.** You can always come down, but you can never go up on price. (When we get to Ending Sales Negotiating Gambits, I'll show you how to Nibble for more. Some things *are* easier to get at the end of the negotiation than they are at the beginning.) What you should be asking for is your MPP—your maximum plausible position. This is the most that you can ask for and still have the buyer see some plausibility in your position.

The less you know about the other side, the higher your initial position should be, for two reasons. First, you may be off in your assumptions. If you don't know the buyer or his needs well, he may be willing to pay more than you think. The second reason is that, if this is a new relationship, you'll appear much more cooperative if you're able to make larger concessions. The better you know the buyer and his needs, the more you can modify your position. Conversely, if the people on the other side don't know you, their initial demands may also be more outrageous.

If you're asking for far more than your maximum plausible position, imply some flexibility. If your initial position seems outrageous to the buyer, and your attitude is "take it or leave it," you may not even get the negotiations started. The buyer's response may simply be, "Then we don't have anything to talk about." However, you can get away with an outrageous opening position if you imply some flexibility. You might say, "We may be able to modify this position once we know your needs more precisely, but based on what we know so far about the quantities you'd be ordering, the quality of the packaging and your needs for just-in-time inventory, our best price would be about $2.25 per widget." At that the buyer will probably be thinking, "That's outrageous, but she does seem flexible, so I'll spend some time negotiating with her and see how low I can get her to go."

Here's the problem for you as a salesperson. Your real MPP is probably much higher than you think it is. We all fear being ridiculed by the other side (which is something that I'll talk more about later when we discuss Coercive Power). We're all reluctant to take a position that will cause the buyer to laugh at us or put us down. So, over the years you have probably modified your MPP to the point where you're asking for less than the maximum price that the buyer would think is plausible.

**The second reason for asking for more than you expect to get will be obvious to you if you're a positive thinker: You might just get it!** You don't know how the universe is aligned that day. Perhaps the spiritual guardian of salespeople is leaning over a cloud looking down at you and thinking, "Wow, look at that salesperson for XYZ Industries. She's been working so hard for so long now, let's just give her a break!" So, you might just get what you ask for.

**The third reason to ask for more than you expect to get is that it raises the perceived value of your product or service.** When you show the buyer your printed price list, it imparts in his or her mind a subliminal value that he or she attaches to the item. Obviously, the effect is greater with an inexperienced buyer than it is with a seasoned pro, but the effect is always there. Let's explore that for a moment. Let's take the case of aspirin.

Everybody knows that aspirin is aspirin. There is no difference between the popular name brand and the private label brands that you pick up in the chain drug stores. So, if I tell you that the brand name costs $2 and the private label costs $1, which would you pick? I would assume the lower priced one.

Now what if I told you that the brand name is on sale, today only, for $1.25? You're probably wavering on your decision. You know that both aspirins are the same, but now it's only a 25-cent difference and it does seem to be a bargain.

Let's add one more thing. What if I gave you a reason for the brand name being more expensive? What if I told you that I believe that they make the brand name to higher quality control standards than the private label? Note that I haven't said that it's made to higher quality control standards, just that I believe it is. Neither have I said that higher quality control standards would make a difference, even if it were true. The difference may be so slight that nobody would ever know the difference or be affected by the difference. However, now you're probably willing to pay 25 percent more for the brand-name aspirin simply because I implanted the higher price in your mind and gave you a reason for it. So, I don't want to hear you telling me that you can't ask for more because your competition sells the same thing for less. If the big drug companies can create the perception that their aspirin is better, you can also create the perception that your product is better. One of the best ways to do this is to ask for a higher price. So, the third reason for asking for more than you expect to get is that it raises the perceived value of the product or service.

**The fourth reason is that it's a great strategy for avoiding deadlocks caused by the conflicting egos of the negotiators.** Look at the Persian Gulf War. (Do you remember the Persian Gulf War—it was on CNN?) What were we asking Saddam Hussein to do back in 1991? President George Bush, in his State of the Union Address, described our opening negotiating position by using a beautiful piece of alliteration (probably written by Peggy Noonan). He said, "I'm not bragging, I'm not bluffing, and I'm not bullying. There are three things this man has to do. He has to get out of Kuwait. He has to restore the legitimate government of Kuwait (don't do what the Soviets did in Afghanistan and install a puppet government). And he has to make reparations for the damage that he's done." That was a very clear and precise opening negotiating position.

The problem was that this was also our bottom line. It was also the least for which we would settle. No wonder the situation deadlocked! It had to deadlock because we didn't give Saddam Hussein room to preserve his ego.

If we'd have said, "Okay. We want you and all your cronies exiled. We want a non-Arab neutral government installed in Baghdad. We want UN supervision of the removal of all military equipment. In addition, we want you out of Kuwait, the legitimate Kuwaiti government restored, and reparation for the damages that you did." Then we could have gotten what we wanted and still let Saddam Hussein salvage his ego.

I know what you're thinking. You're thinking, "Roger, Saddam Hussein was not on my Christmas card list last year. I don't care if his ego deflates like a balloon that's been stuck with a hat pin." I agree with that! However, it creates a problem in negotiation. It creates deadlocks.

From the Persian Gulf scenario, you could draw one of two conclusions. The first possibility is that our State Department negotiators are complete blithering idiots! What's the second possibility? Right! That this was a situation where we wanted to create a deadlock because it served our purpose.

We had no intention of settling for just the three things that George Bush asked for in his State of the Union Address. General

Schwarzkopf in his biography, *It Doesn't Take a Hero,* said, "The minute we got there, we understood that anything less than a military victory was a defeat for the United States." We couldn't let Saddam Hussein pull 600,000 troops back across the border, leaving us wondering when he would choose to do it again. We had to have a reason to go in and take care of him militarily.

So, that was a situation where it served our purpose to create a deadlock. What concerns me is that when you're making a presentation to a buyer, you are inadvertently creating a deadlock because you don't have the courage to ask for more than you expect to get.

**There's a fifth reason to ask for more than you expect to get, and it's the reason Power Sales Negotiators say that you should do it: It's the only way that you can create a climate where the buyer feels that he or she won.** If you go in with your best offer up front, there's no way buyers can negotiate with you and feel that they won.

Inexperienced negotiators always want to start with their best offer. This is the salesperson who is saying to the sales manager, "I'm going out on this big proposal today, and I know that it's going to be competitive. I know that they're getting bids from people all over town. Let me cut the price up front, or we won't stand a chance of getting the order." Power Sales Negotiators know the value of asking for more than you expect to get. It's one of the key ways that you can create a climate where buyers feel that they won.

In highly publicized negotiations, such as when the baseball players or airline pilots go on strike, the initial demands that both sides make are outrageous. I remember being involved in a union negotiation where I could barely believe the initial demands. The demand of the union was to triple the wages of the employees. The opening demand of the company was to make it an open shop. In other words, a voluntary union that would have the effect of destroying the power of the union at that location. However, Power Sales Negotiators know that the initial demands in these types of negotiations are always extreme, so they don't let it bother them. They know that as the negotiations progress, they will work their way in toward the middle where they will find a solution with which both sides can live. Then they can both call a press conference and announce that they won in the negotiations. So, particularly with egotistical buyers always leave some room to let them have a win.

*Power Sales Negotiators always ask for more than they expect to get.*

Let's recap the five reasons for asking for more than you expect to get:

1. It gives you some negotiating room. You can always come down but you can never go up.
2. You might just get it.
3. It raises the perceived value of your product or service.
4. It avoids deadlocks caused by the conflicting egos of the negotiators.
5. It creates a climate where the other side can win.

## Asking for More Than You Expect to Get: A Fable

There was once an old couple who lived in a dilapidated thatched hut on a remote Pacific Island. One day a hurricane blew through the village, demolishing their home. Because they were much too old and poor to rebuild the hut, the couple moved in with their daughter and her husband. This arrangement precipitated an unpleasant domestic situation because the daughter's hut was barely big enough for herself, her husband, and their four children, let alone the in-laws.

The daughter went to the wise person of the village and asked, "Whatever will we do?"

The wise person puffed slowly on a pipe and then responded, "You have chickens, don't you?"

"Yes," she replied, "we have 10 chickens."

"Then bring the chickens into the hut with you."

This seemed ludicrous to the daughter, but she followed the wise person's advice. The move naturally exacerbated the problem, and the situation was soon unbearable, as feathers as well as hostile words flew around the hut. The daughter returned to the wise person, pleading again for advice.

"You have pigs, do you not?" asked the wise person.

"Yes, we have three pigs."

"Then you must bring the pigs into your hut with you."

That seemed to be ridiculous advice, but to question the wise person was unthinkable, so she brought the pigs into the hut. Life was now truly unlivable, with eight people, 10 chickens, and three pigs sharing one tiny, noisy hut. Her husband was complaining that he couldn't hear CNN over the racket.

The next day the daughter, fearing for her family's sanity, approached the wise person with a final desperate plea. "Please," she cried, "we cannot live like this. Tell me what to do and I'll do it, but please help us!"

This time the wise person's response was puzzling, but easier to follow. "Now remove the chickens and the pigs from your hut."

She quickly evicted the animals and the entire family lived happily together for the rest of their days.

The moral of the story is that a deal always looks better after you have thrown something out!

Ask for more than you expect to get. It seems like such an obvious principle, but it's something that you can virtually count on in a negotiation. In thousands of workshop situations and in tens of thousands of traceable real life situations, this is something that has proven itself repeatedly. The more you ask for, the more you're going to get.

**The Counter Gambit.** When a buyer asks *you* for more than he expects to get, you should recognize the Gambit, appeal to his sense of fair play, and use Higher Authority and Good Guy/Bad Guy (two Gambits that I'll teach you later). You should say, "Of course you could open the negotiation at any figure you choose, and I could respond with an equally outrageous proposal, but neither of us would benefit from that approach. Why don't you tell me the highest price you can live with, and I'll take it to my people and see what I can do for you with them. Fair enough?"

# Key points to remember

➢ Ask for more than you expect to get. You may just get it, and it gives you some negotiating room. Most important, it creates a climate where the other side can win.

➢ Your objective should be to advance your MPP—your maximum plausible position.

➢ If your initial proposal is extreme, imply some flexibility. This encourages the buyer to negotiate with you.

➤ The less you know about the other side, the more you should ask for. A stranger is more likely to surprise you, and you can build goodwill by making bigger concessions.

➤ Counter by appealing to the buyer's sense of fair play and using Higher Authority and Good Guy/Bad Guy.

In Chapter 5, I'll teach you how to figure out how much more than you're expecting to get you should ask for.

# Chapter 5

# Bracketing

In Chapter 4, I taught you why you should always ask for more than you expect to get. The next question has to be: If you're asking for more than you expect to get, how much more than you expect to get should you ask for? The answer is that you should *bracket* your objective. Your initial proposal should be an equal distance on the other side of your objective as their proposal.

Let me give you a simple example of that. The buyer is offering you $1.60 for your widgets. You can live with $1.70. Bracketing tells you that you should start at $1.80. Then if you end up in the middle, you'll still make your objective.

Of course it's not always true that you'll end up in the middle, but that is a good assumption to make if you don't have anything to go on. Assume that you'll end up in the middle, mid-way between the two opening negotiating positions. If you track that, you will be amazed how often it happens—in little things and in big things.

**In little things.** Your son comes to you and says he needs $20 for a fishing trip he's going to take this weekend. You say, "No way! I'm not going to give you $20. Do you realize that when I was your age I got 50 cents a week allowance, and I had to work for that? I'll give you $10 and not a penny more."

Your son says, "I can't do it for $10!"

Now you have established the negotiating range. He's asking for $20. You're willing to pay $10. See how often you end up at $15! In our culture, splitting the difference always seems fair.

**In big things.** In 1982, Treasury Secretary Donald Regan and Federal Reserve Board Chairman Paul Volcker were negotiating the pay off of a huge international loan with the government of Mexico. Mexico was about to default on an $82-billion dollar loan. Their chief negotiator was Jesus Herzog, their finance minister. In a creative solution, they agreed to contribute huge amounts of petroleum to our strategic petroleum reserve. However, that didn't settle it all. We proposed to the Mexicans that they pay us a $100-million dollar negotiating fee, which was a politically acceptable way for them to pay us accrued interest. When President Lopez Portillo heard what we were asking for, he went ballistic. He said the equivalent of: You tell Ronald Reagan to drop dead. We're not paying the United States a negotiating fee. Not one peso! Nada!

So, here we have the negotiating range established. We're asking for $100 million dollars. They're offering zero. Guess what they ended up paying us? That's right. Fifty million dollars.

Often, in little things and in big things, we end up splitting the difference. With bracketing, Power Sales Negotiators are assured that if that happens, they still get what they want.

Bracketing assumes one thing: that you can get the other side to state his or her position first. If buyers get you to state your position first, they can bracket you so that if you end up splitting the difference, as so often happens, the buyers end up getting what they want. That's an underlying principle of negotiating. Get the other side to state a position first. This is necessary so that you can bracket that proposal.

Don't let the other side trick you into committing first. If the status quo is fine with you, and there is no pressure on you to make a move, be bold enough to say to the other side, "You're the one who approached me. The way things are satisfies me. If you want to do this, you'll have to make a proposal to me."

Some crafty negotiators go to incredible lengths to make it look as though the other side approached them when the reverse is true. Movie producer Sam Goldwyn once wanted to borrow a contract actor from Darryl Zanuck, but couldn't reach Zanuck because he was in a meeting. After many tries to reach Zanuck, an exasperated Goldwyn finally insisted that the call be put through. When Zanuck finally picked up the phone, Goldwyn, who had initiated the call, said, "Darryl, what can I do for you today?"

If Paul McCartney and The Beatles had learned to avoid making the first offer, he'd be even richer today. In the early days of the group, their manager Brian Epstein was negotiating a contract for their first movie. United Artists had planned it as a teenage exploitation movie and budgeted only $300,000. The producer offered Epstein $25,000 and a percentage of the profits. United Artists was willing to pay up to 25 percent of the profits if the Beatles would agree to the token cash payment, but he was a good enough negotiator to play his hand close to his vest. Without revealing his position, he asked Brian Epstein what he wanted first. Brian was not used to big numbers yet and furthermore hadn't taken the time to research the industry. He assertively replied that he wouldn't accept a penny less than 7.5 percent. The movie *A Hard Day's Night* was an international success and Brian's error of making the first offer cost the Beatles millions of dollars.

After your buyer states a position, you can bracket your position on the high side of your objective—it's best to do this with implied flexibility. Your price may be high but when you indicate a willingness to negotiate, the buyer has a tendency to think, "It sounds as though we can get her down from that. Why don't I spend some time and see if I can get her down to a lower price than I'm paying now." It's a good way to get the negotiations started.

**The Counter Gambit.** You can stop a buyer from bracketing you by getting him to commit to a position first.

## Key points to remember

➤ Bracket a proposal so that if you end up splitting the difference, you still get what you want.
➤ You can only bracket if you get the buyer to state his or her position first.
➤ Continue bracketing as you zero in on your objective with concessions.

# Chapter 6

# Never Say Yes to
# the First Offer

Now let's move on to another major principle that is critical in the beginning stages of the negotiation: **Never say yes to the first offer or counter offer.** The reason that you should never do this is that it automatically triggers two thoughts in the buyer's mind.

Put yourself in the buyer's shoes for a moment. Let's say that you're a buyer for a maker of aircraft engines and you're about to meet with a salesperson who represents the manufacturer of engine bearings, something that's a vital component for you. Your regular supplier has let you down and you need to make an emergency purchase from this new company. They are the only people who can supply within the 30 days that you need to prevent a shut down of your assembly line. If you can't supply the engines on time, it will invalidate your contract with the aircraft manufacturer that gives you 85 percent of your business. Under these circumstances, the price of the bearings you need is definitely not a high priority. However, as your secretary announces the arrival of the salesperson, you think to yourself, "I'll be a good negotiator. Just to see what happens I'll make him a super low offer."

The salesperson makes his presentation and assures you that he can ship on time to your specifications. He quotes you a price of $250 each for the bearings.

This surprises you because you have been paying $275 for them. However, you manage to mask your surprise and respond with, "We've only been paying $175." To which the salesperson responds, "Okay, we can match that."

In the thousands of seminars that I've conducted over the years, I've posed a situation such as this to audiences and can't recall getting anything other than these two responses:

1. I could have done better.
2. Something must be wrong.

**First Reaction: I could have done better.** The interesting thing about this is that it doesn't have a thing to do with the price. It has to do only with the way the other person reacts to the proposal. What if that bearing salesperson had agreed to $150 or $125? Wouldn't you still think you could have done better?

Several years ago, I bought 100 acres of land in Eatonville, Washington—a beautiful little town just west of Mount Rainier. The seller was asking $185,000 for the land. I analyzed the property and decided that if I could get it for $150,000, it would be a terrific buy. So, I bracketed that price and asked the real estate agent to present an offer to the seller at $115,050. (Specific numbers build credibility, so you're more likely to get them to accept an offer such as this than have them counter at a higher price.)

I went back to La Habra Heights, California, where I live, leaving the agent to present the offer to the seller. Frankly, I thought I'd be lucky if they responded at all to a proposal this low. To my amazement, I got the offer back in the mail a few days later, and they had accepted the price and terms that I had proposed. I know that I got a terrific buy on the land. Within a year, I'd sold 60 of the acres for more than I paid for the whole hundred. Later I sold another 20 acres for more than I paid for the whole 100. So, when they accepted my offer I should have been thinking, "Wow. That's terrific, I couldn't have gotten a lower price." That's what I should have been thinking, but I wasn't. I was thinking, "I could have done better." So, it doesn't have anything to do with the price—it has to do only with the way the other side reacts to the proposal.

**Second Reaction: Something must be wrong.** My second reaction when I received the accepted offer on the land was, "Something must be wrong. I'm going to take a thorough look at the preliminary title report when it comes in. Something must be going on that I don't understand if they're willing to accept an offer that I didn't think they would."

The second thought that the buyer of the bearings will have is, "Something must be wrong. Maybe something's changed in the market since I last negotiated a bearing contract. Instead of going ahead, I think I'll tell this salesperson that I've got to check with a committee and then talk to some other suppliers."

Those two reactions will go through anybody's mind if you say yes to the first offer. Let's say your son came to you and said, "Could I borrow the car tonight?" and you said, "Sure son, take it. Have a wonderful time." Wouldn't he automatically think, "I could have done better. I could have gotten $10 for the movie out of this." And wouldn't he automatically think, "What's going on here? How come they want me out of the house? What's going on that I don't understand?"

This is a very easy negotiating principle to understand but it's very hard to remember when you're in the thick of a negotiation. You may have formed a mental picture of how you expect the buyer to respond, and that's a dangerous thing to do. Napoleon Bonaparte once said, "The unforgivable sin of a commander is to 'form a picture'—to assume that the enemy will act a certain way in a given situation, when his response may be altogether different." So, you're expecting them to counter at a ridiculously low figure and to your surprise, the buyer's proposal is much more reasonable than you expected it to be. For example:

➤ You sell vacuum cleaners to department store chains. You know that the buyer will expect you to contribute advertising money to their Labor Day mailer, and you're expecting them to ask for $25,000. You have only $20,000 left in your advertising fund. To your surprise, they ask only for $10,000. There's a real danger that you'll say yes too quickly.

➤ You sell MRI (magnetic resoning imaging) equipment to hospitals. Your list price is $1.2 million, but you typically end up selling it for $900,000. City Hospital has been getting bids from every supplier in the business and you have every reason to believe that you're going to have to sell at rock bottom price to get their order. So, you're expecting them to counter at $800,000, if you're lucky. To your amazement, they come back at $950,000. There's a real danger that you'll say yes too quickly.

> ➢ You lease fleets of cars and you've been trying to get the business of a huge engineering company. Finally, they make a proposal to you. They want to lease 300 cars and 400 light trucks. You're expecting them to propose 6 percent under invoice. To your surprise, they come back at only 4.5 percent under invoice, well within your negotiating range. There's a real danger that you'll say yes too quickly.

So, Power Sales Negotiators are careful that they don't fall into the trap of saying yes too quickly, which would automatically trigger these two thoughts in the buyer's mind:

1. I could have done better. (And next time I will! A sophisticated buyer won't tell you he felt that he lost in the negotiation. But he will tuck it away in the back of his mind, thinking, "The next time I deal with this salesperson I'll be a tougher negotiator. I won't leave any money on the table next time.")
2. Something must be wrong.

Turning down the first offer may be tough to do, particularly if you've been calling on the buyer for months and just as you're about to give up, they come through with a proposal. It will tempt you to grab what you can. When this happens, be a Power Sales Negotiator—remember not to say yes too quickly.

Many years ago, I was president of a real estate company in Southern California with 28 offices and 540 sales associates. One day, a magazine salesperson tried to sell me advertising space in his magazine. I was familiar with the magazine and knew it to be an excellent opportunity so I wanted my company to be in it. He made me a very reasonable proposal that required a modest $2,000 investment. Because I love to negotiate, I started using some Gambits on him and got him down to the incredibly low price of $800. You can imagine what I was thinking at that point. Right! I was thinking, "Holy cow! If I got him down from $2,000 to $800 in just a few minutes, I wonder how low I can get him to go if I keep on negotiating?" So, I used a Middle Gambit on him called Higher Authority. I said, "This looks fine. I do just have to run it by my board of directors. Fortunately, they're meeting tonight. Let me run it by them and get back to you with the final okay."

The next day I called him back and said, "I'm so embarrassed about this. I felt sure that I could sell the board on the $800 price you quoted me, but they're so difficult to deal with right now. The budget's been giving everyone headaches lately. They did come back with a counter offer, but it's so low that it embarrasses me to even tell you what it is."

There was a long pause and he finally said, "How much did they agree to?"

"$500."

"That's okay, I'll take it," he said—and I felt cheated. Although I'd negotiated him down from $2,000 to $500, I still felt that I could have done better!

There's a postscript to this story. I'm always reluctant to tell stories such as this at my seminars for fear that it may get back to the person with whom I was negotiating. However, the following year I was speaking at the huge California Association of Realtors convention, which was being held that year in San Diego. I told this story in my talk, never imagining that the magazine salesperson was standing in the back of the room. As I finished my presentation, I saw him pushing his way through the crowd. I braced myself for what I expected to be a verbal assault.

However, he shook my hand and said with a smile, "I can't thank you enough for explaining that to me. I had no idea the impact that my tendency to jump at a quick deal was having on people. I'll never do that again."

I used to think that it was a 100-percent rule that you should never say yes to the first offer. Until I heard from a real estate office manager in Los Angeles who told me, "I was driving down Hollywood Boulevard last night, listening to your cassette tapes in my car. I stopped at a gas station to use the rest room. When I came back to my car, somebody stuck a gun in my ribs and said, 'Okay buddy. Give me your wallet.' Well, I'd just been listening to your tapes, so I said, 'Here's what I'm prepared to do. I'll give you the cash, but let me keep the wallet and the credit cards, fair enough?' And he said, 'Buddy, you didn't listen to me, did you? Give me the wallet!'" So, although there are sometimes when you should say yes to the first offer, it's almost a 100-percent rule that you shouldn't!

**The Counter Gambit.** The way to protect yourself from the Never Jumping at the First Offer Gambit is to protect yourself with Higher Authority. Always be thinking to yourself, "Whatever the buyer's counterproposal may be, I can't accept it. I have to take it to my committee."

## Key points to remember

➤ Never say yes to the first offer or counter offer from the buyer. It automatically triggers two thoughts: "I could have done better (and next time I will)," and "Something must be wrong."

➤ The biggest danger is when you have formed a mental picture of how the buyer will respond to your proposal, and he comes back much higher than you expected. Prepare for this possibility so it won't catch you off guard.

# Chapter 7

# Flinching

Power Sales Negotiators know that you should always **Flinch**—which means to react with shock and surprise at the buyer's proposals.

Let's say that you're in a resort area and stop to watch one of those charcoal sketch artists. He doesn't have the price posted, so you ask him how much he charges and he tells you $15. If that doesn't appear to shock you, his next words will be, "And $5 extra for color." If you still don't appear shocked, he will say, "And we have these shipping cartons here, you'll need one of these too."

Perhaps you know somebody who would never Flinch like that because it's beneath his or her dignity. This is the kind of person who would say to a store clerk, "How much is the coat in the window?"

The clerk responds, "$2,000."

"That's not bad!" he or she would say. A Power Sales Negotiator would be having a heart attack when they hear a price like that!

I know it sounds ridiculous but the truth of the matter is that when buyers make a proposal, they are watching for your reaction. They may not think for a moment that you'll agree to their request. They've just thrown it out to see what your reaction will be. For example:

> ➤ You sell computers and the buyer asks you to include an extended warranty.

> ➤ You sell cars and the buyer asks you to include free floor mats and a full tank of gas.

> ➤ You sell contractor supplies and the buyer asks you to deliver it to the job site at no extra charge.

➢ You sell fax machines and the buyer asks you to include a years' supply of paper.

In each of these situations, the buyer may not have thought for a moment that you would go along with his request, but if you don't Flinch he or she will automatically think, "Maybe I will get them to go along with that. I didn't think they would, but I think I'll be a tough negotiator and see how far I can get them to go.

It is very interesting to observe a negotiation when you know what both sides are thinking. Wouldn't that be fascinating for you? Wouldn't you love to know what's going on in the buyer's mind when you're negotiating with him? When I conduct the Secrets of Power Negotiating seminars, we break up into groups and do some negotiating to practice the principles that I teach. I create a workshop and customize it to the industry in which the participants are involved. If they are medical equipment salespeople, they may find themselves negotiating the sale of laser surgery equipment to a hospital. If they are printing salespeople, the workshop may involve the acquisition of a smaller printing company in an outlying town.

I break the audience up into buyers, sellers, and referees. The referees are in a very interesting position because they have been in on the planning sessions of both the buyers and the sellers. They know each side's negotiating range. They know what the opening offer is going to be, and they know how far each side will go. So, the sellers of the printing company would go as low as $700,000 but they may start as high as $2 million. The buyers may start at $400,000 but they will go to $1.5 million if they have to. We call that the high and low of each side's negotiating range. Hopefully the high end of the buyer's negotiating range is more than the low end of the seller's negotiating range. The acceptance range is the extent to which the two ranges overlap. So, the combined negotiating range of the buyers and sellers is $400,000 to $2 million, but the acceptance range is $700,000 to $1.5 million.

The negotiating starts with each side trying to get the other side to put their offer on the table first. After awhile, someone has to break the ice, so the sellers may suggest the $2 million that is the top of their negotiating range.

To them, $2 million is ridiculously high and they barely have the nerve to propose it. They think they're going to get laughed out of the room if they do. But to their surprise, the buyers don't appear shocked because they didn't Flinch at the proposal. They expect the buyers to Flinch with shock and surprise and exclaim, "You want us to do what? You must be out of your minds!" However, they don't Flinch and their response is much milder, perhaps, "We don't think we'd be prepared to go that high." In an instant, the negotiation changes. A moment ago, the $2 million had seemed to be an impossible goal. Now, because the buyer's didn't Flinch, the sellers are thinking that perhaps they're not as far apart as they thought they were. Now they're thinking, "Let's hang in. Let's be tough negotiators. Maybe we can get this much."

Flinching is critical because most people believe more what they see than what they hear. The visual overrides the auditory in most people. It's safe to assume that at least 70 percent of your buyers will be visuals. What they see is more important than what they hear. I'm sure you've had some exposure to neuro-linguistic programming. You know that people are either visual, auditory, or kinesthetic (what they feel is paramount). If you'd like to know whether you are a visual, an auditory, or a kinesthetic, I can teach you in 10 seconds.

I want you to close your eyes and think of the house in which you lived when you were 10 years old. Do that now and then I'll tell you what it means.

Here's how to judge your reaction to that experience. When you thought about the house in which you lived when you were 10, you either saw the house in your mind, or you got an auditory cue (you heard something in your mind), or you revisited feelings that you had when you lived there.

You probably saw the house in your mind, so you're a visual. Perhaps you didn't get a good visual picture, but you heard what was going on—perhaps trains passing by or children playing. That means you're auditory. Some auditories are very auditory. Neil Berman is a psychotherapist friend of mine in Santa Fe, New Mexico. He can remember every conversation he's ever had with all his patients, but if he meets them in the supermarket, he doesn't remember them. The minute they say good morning to him and he hears their voice, he thinks, "Oh yes, that's the bipolar personality with antisocial tendencies." The third possibility is that you didn't so much see or hear, but you got a feeling for what it was like when you were 10. That makes you a kinesthetic.

Assume that people are visual unless you have something else to go on. This means they will react to a Flinch in response to a proposal.

Do not dismiss Flinching as childish or too theatrical until you'd had a chance to see how effective it can be. The effectiveness of Flinching always surprises my students when they first use it. A woman told me that she Flinched when selecting a bottle of wine in one of Boston's finest restaurants and the wine steward immediately dropped the price by five dollars. A man told me that a simple Flinch caused the salesperson to take $2,000 off the price of a Corvette.

A speaker friend of mine attended my seminar in Orange County, California, and decided to see if he could use it to get his speaking fees up. At the time he was just getting started and was charging $1,500. He went to a company and proposed that they hire him to do some in-house training. The training director said, "We might be interested in having you work for us, but the most we can pay you is $1,500."

In the past he would have said, "That's what I charge." But now he gasped in surprise and said, "$1,500! I couldn't afford to do it for just $1,500."

The training director frowned thoughtfully. "Well," he said, "the most we've ever offered any speaker is $2,500, so that's the very best we can do." That meant $1,000 of additional bottom-line profit dollars per speech to my friend and it only took him 15 seconds to do. Not bad pay!

**The Counter Gambit.** If someone pulls a Flinch on you first, the best thing to do is to smile and recognize the Gambit: "That was a terrific Flinch! Where did you learn how to do that?" If she tells you that it was from reading this book, you'll have a lot in common, won't you?

# Key points to remember

> Flinch in reaction to a proposal from the buyer. They may not expect to get what they're asking for, and if you don't show surprise, you're communicating that it's a possibility.
> A concession often follows a Flinch. If you don't Flinch, it makes the buyer a tougher negotiator.
> Assume that the buyer is a visual person unless you have something else to go on.
> Even if you're not face-to-face with the buyer, you should still gasp in shock and surprise, because telephone flinches can also be very effective.

## Chapter 8

# Playing Reluctant Seller

Now let me teach you how to **Play Reluctant Seller** and defend yourself against the Reluctant Buyer. Imagine for a moment that you own a sailboat and you're desperate to sell it. It was fun when you first got it but now you hardly ever use it and the maintenance and slip fees are eating you alive. It's early Sunday morning and you've given up a chance to play golf with your buddies because you need to be down at the marina cleaning your boat. You're scrubbing away and cursing your stupidity for even having bought the boat. Just as you're thinking, "I'm going to give this turkey away to the next person who comes along," you look up and see an expensively dressed silver-haired man with a young girl on his arm coming down the dock. He's wearing Gucci loafers, white slacks, and a blue Burberry's blazer topped off with a silk cravat. His young girlfriend is wearing high heels, a silk sheath dress, big sunglasses, and huge diamond earrings.

They stop at your boat and the man says, "That's a fine looking boat, young man. By any chance is it for sale?"

His girlfriend snuggles up to him and says, "Oh let's buy it, poopsy. We'll have so much fun."

You feel your heart start to burst with joy and your mind is singing, "Thank you! Thank you!"

Expressing that sentiment is not going to get you the best price for your boat, is it? How are you going to get the best price? By playing Reluctant Seller. You keep on scrubbing and say, "You're welcome to come aboard, although I hadn't thought of selling the boat." You give them a tour of the boat and at every step of the way you tell them how much you love the boat and how much fun you have sailing her. Finally you tell them, "I can see how perfect this boat would be for you and how much fun you'd have with it, but I really don't think I could ever bear to part with it. However, just to be fair to you, what is the very best price you would give me?"

Power Sales Negotiators know that this Reluctant Seller technique squeezes the negotiating range before the negotiating even starts. If you've done a good job of building the other person's desire to own the boat, he will have already formed a negotiating range in his mind. He may be thinking, "I'd be willing to go to $30,000; $25,000 would be a fair deal; and $20,000 would be a bargain." So, his negotiating range is from $20,000 to $30,000. Just by playing Reluctant Seller, you will have moved him up through that range. If you had appeared eager to sell, he may have offered you $20,000. By playing Reluctant Seller you may move him to the mid-point or even the high point of his negotiating range, before the negotiations even start.

One of my Power Negotiators is an extremely rich and powerful investor, a man who owns real estate all over town. He probably owns real estate worth $50 million, owes $35 million in loans, and therefore has a net worth of about $15 million. He likes wheeling and dealing. He's very successful—what you could justifiably call a heavy hitter. Like many investors, his strategy is simple: Buy a property at the right price and on the right terms, hold onto it and let it appreciate, then sell at a higher price. Many smaller investors bring him purchase offers for one of his holdings, eager to acquire one of his better-known properties, and when that happens he always uses the Reluctant Seller Gambit. He reads the offer quietly and when he's finished he slides it thoughtfully back across the table saying, "I don't know. Of all my properties, I have very special feelings for this one. I was thinking of keeping it and giving it to my daughter for her college graduation present, and I really don't think that I would part with it for anything less than the full asking price. You understand; this particular property is worth a great deal to me. But look, it was good of you to bring in an offer for me, and in all fairness, so that you won't have wasted your time, what is the very best price you would give me?" Many times, I saw him make thousands of dollars in just a few seconds using the Reluctant Seller philosophy.

Power Sales Negotiators always try to edge up the other side's negotiating range before the real negotiating ever begins.

I remember an ocean front condo I bought as an investment. The owner was asking $59,000 for it. It was a hot real estate market at the time and I wasn't sure how eager the owner was to sell, or if she had any other offers on it. So, I wrote up three offers, one at $49,000, another at $54,000, and a third at $59,000. I made an appointment to meet with the seller, who had moved out of the condominium in Long Beach and was now living in Pasadena. After talking to her for a while, I determined that she hadn't had any other offers and that she was very eager to sell. Because she didn't play the role of Reluctant Seller, I reached into my briefcase, where I had the three offers carefully filed, and pulled out the lowest of them. She accepted it immediately and when I sold the condominium a few years later, it fetched $129,000.

Power Sales Negotiators should always play Reluctant Seller when they're selling to squeeze the negotiating range before the negotiation even starts.

Now let's turn this around and consider the Reluctant Buyer. Put yourself on the other side of the desk for a moment. If you were the purchasing agent, how would you get a salesperson to give you the lowest possible price? If I were a purchasing agent, I would let the buyer come in and have her go through her entire presentation.

I would ask all the questions I could possibly think of, and when I finally couldn't think of another thing to ask, I would say, "I really appreciate all the time you've taken. You've obviously put a lot of work into this presentation but, unfortunately, it's just not the way we want to go. But I sure wish you the best of luck." The salesperson would look disappointed. She would slowly package up her presentation materials and start to leave. Then at the very last moment, just as her hand hit the doorknob on the way out, I would come back with this magic expression. (There are some magic expressions in negotiating. If you use them at exactly the right moment, the predictability of the other side's response is amazing.) I would say, "You know, I really do appreciate the time you took with me. Just to be fair to you, what is the very lowest price that you would take?"

Would you agree with me that it's a good bet that the first price the salesperson quoted is not the real bottom-line? Sure it's a good bet. The first price a salesperson quotes is what I call the "wish number." This is what he is wishing the buyer would take. If the buyer said okay to that, he would probably burn rubber all the way back to the sales office and run in screaming, "You can't believe what just happened to me! I was over at XYZ Company to make a bid on the furniture they need for their new headquarters. I went over the proposal and they said, 'What's your absolute bottom-line price?' I was feeling good so I said, 'We never budge off list price less a quantity discount, so the bottom-line is $225,000,' and held my breath. The president said, 'It sounds high, but if that's the best you can do, go ahead and ship it.' I can't believe it! Let's close the office and go celebrate!" So, the first price quoted is what I call the wish price.

Somewhere out there, there's a walk-away price. A price at which the salesperson will not or cannot sell. The buyer doesn't know what the walk-away price is, so he or she has to do some probing, some seeking of information. He or she has to try some negotiating Gambits to figure out the salesperson's walk-away price.

When the purchasing agent plays Reluctant Buyer, the salesperson is not going to come all the way from the wish price to the walk-away price. However, here's what will typically happen. When the purchasing agent plays Reluctant Buyer, the salesperson will typically give away half of her negotiating range. If that furniture salesperson knows that his bottom-line is $175,000, $50,000 below the list price, he will typically respond to the Reluctant Buyer Gambit with, "Well, I tell you what. It's the end of our quarter and we're in a sales contest. If you'll place the order today, I'll give it to you for the unbelievably low price of $200,000." He'll give away half of his negotiating range, just because the purchasing agent played Reluctant Buyer.

**The Counter Gambit.** When you meet a Reluctant Buyer, say, "I don't think there's any flexibility in the price, but if you'll tell me what it would take to get your business *(getting the other side to commit first),* I'll take it to my people *(Higher Authority—a Middle Negotiating Gambit I'll cover later)* and I'll see what I can do for you with them *(Good Guy/Bad Guy—an Ending Negotiating Gambit)."* Power Sales Negotiators don't get upset by a Reluctant Buyer/Seller. They just learn to play the negotiating game better than the buyer.

# Key points to remember

➢ Always play Reluctant Seller.

➢ Look out for the Reluctant Buyer.

➢ Playing this Gambit is a great way to squeeze the other side's negotiating range before the negotiation even starts.

➢ The other side will typically give away half of their negotiating range just because you use this technique.

---

# Chapter 9

# Concentrate on the Issues

It is critical for you to remember during the beginning stage of the negotiation that you should always **Concentrate on the Issues** and not get thrown off by the actions of the other negotiator.

Have you ever watched tennis on television and seen a highly emotional star like John McEnroe, jumping up and down at the other end of the court? You wonder to yourself, "How on earth can anybody play tennis against somebody like that? It's such a game of concentration it doesn't seem fair."

The answer is that good tennis players understand that only one thing affects the outcome of the game of tennis. That's the movement of the ball across the net. What the other player is doing doesn't affect the outcome of the game at all, as long as you know what the ball is doing. So, in that way, tennis players learn to concentrate on the ball, not on the other person.

When you're negotiating, the ball is the movement of the goal concessions across the negotiating table. It's the only thing that affects the outcome of the game, but it's so easy to get thrown off by what the other people are doing, isn't it?

I remember once being interested in acquiring a large real estate project in Signal Hill, California, that comprised 18 four-unit buildings. However, I knew that I had to get the price down way below the $1.8 million that the sellers were asking for the property. A large group of real estate investors owned the project free and clear. A real estate agent had brought it to my attention, so I felt obligated to let him present the first offer, reserving the right to go back and negotiate directly with the sellers if he wasn't able to get my $1.2 million offer accepted.

The last thing in the world the agent wanted to do was present an offer at $1.2 million—$600,000 below the asking price, but finally I persuaded him to try, and off he went to present the offer. He made a tactical error here. He shouldn't have gone to them; he should have had them come to him. You always have more control when you're negotiating in your own power base than if you go to their power base.

He came back a few hours later and I said, "How did it go?"

"It was awful, just awful. I'm so embarrassed." He told me. "I got into this large conference room where all of the principals had come in for the reading of the offer. Their attorney, their CPA, and their real estate broker were all there. I was planning to do the silent close on them." (Which is to read the offer and let the next person who talks lose in the negotiations.) "The problem was, there wasn't any silence. I got down to the $1.2 million and they said: 'Wait a minute. You're coming in $600,000 low? We're insulted!' Then they all got up and stormed out of the room."

I said, "Nothing else happened?"

He said, "Well, a couple of the principals stopped in the doorway on their way out and they said: 'We're not going to come down to a penny less than $1.5 million.' It was just awful! Please don't ever ask me to present an offer that low again."

I said, "Wait a minute. You mean to tell me that, in five minutes, you got them to come down $300,000, and you feel bad about the way the negotiations went?" He was distracted by their actions and lost sight of the deal.

A clients told me a great story about getting distracted from the real issues in a negotiation. He told me that many years ago, he had proudly expanded his company into a huge new facility. He tried to find a buyer for his old warehouse but didn't have any luck. He had put the property on the market for $3.3 million but the only offer he got was for $900,000, which he reluctantly accepted. However, at the last moment, the buyer backed out and he was back to square one.

A few weeks later a friend of his told him about a company that was looking for a warehouse and that company agreed to buy the warehouse for $3 million. As he walked through the property with the new buyer, he explained that all of the metal desks and cabinets would be included, but the wooden desks were not because he intended to move them to his new facility. The buyer agreed to this but later insisted that my client had told him that all of the desks were included in the sale.

My client became furious that the buyer was accusing him of lying about the desks. The argument became so intense that it looked as though the whole sale was going to fall apart. Fortunately, my client's brother saw them arguing and called his brother aside. "Look, it's your warehouse and you can do what you want with it," he told his brother. "But may I point out to you that last month you were willing to sell it for $900,000. Now you have a buyer willing to pay $3 million, and you're about to upset him over a few thousand dollars worth of used furniture." With that my client retrieved his perspective and gracefully conceded that the wooden desks would be included in the sale.

See how easy it is to be thrown off by what the other people are doing, rather than concentrating on the issues in a negotiation? It's inconceivable that a full-time professional negotiator, say an international negotiator, would walk out of negotiations because he doesn't think the other people are fair. He may walk out, but it's a specific negotiating tactic, not because he's upset.

Can you imagine a top arms negotiator walking out on Russian negotiations and saying to the PRESIDENT, "Those guys are so unfair. You can't trust them, and they never keep their commitments. I got so upset, I just walked out"? Power Sales Negotiators don't do that. They concentrate on the issues, not on the personalities. You should always be thinking, "Where are we now, compared to where we were an hour ago, or yesterday, or last week?"

President Clinton's Secretary of State, Warren Christopher, said, "It's okay to get upset when you're negotiating, as long as you're in control and you're doing it as a specific negotiating tactic." It's when you're genuinely upset and out of control that you always lose.

That's why salespeople will have this happen to them. They lose an account. They take it into their sales manager and they say, "Well, we lost this one. Don't waste any time trying to save it. I did everything I could. If anybody could have saved it, I would have saved it."

So, the sales manager says, "Well, just as a public relations gesture, let me give them a call anyway." The sales manager can hold it together, not necessarily because he's any brighter or sharper than the salesperson, but because he hasn't become emotionally involved with the people the way the salesperson has. Don't do that. Learn to concentrate on the issues.

**The Counter Gambit** to getting emotionally involved is to think of any emotional outburst as a negotiating tactic on the part of the buyer. Let's say that you're calling on your favorite customer who is the buyer at a small chain of retail outlets. Normally you have a good time together, but not this time. This time he's furious at you, the minute you walk through the door. He's waiving a page of a newspaper and flapping it so fast in your face that you have trouble seeing what he's talking about. Finally, after several minutes of his ranting and raving, you understand the problem. One of his competitors has advertised your best-selling product at an exceptionally low price. So, the buyer is convinced that you've given them a lower cost than you've ever offered him. This outburst could trigger several visceral reactions, including:

➤ Oh no! I goofed!

➤ I can't believe he's pulling this on me.

➤ The idiot! He knows that I made him the same offer and he turned it down.

➤ I'm in serious trouble if I lose this account over this one.

None of these reactions are the reactions of a Power Sales Negotiator. You should be calmly thinking, "This is a negotiating ploy that he's using on me. He's not really upset. He's doing this to get something from me. What is it he wants and how should I react?" By thinking of his outburst as a calculated negotiating gambit, rather than an emotional outburst, you will stop yourself from getting emotionally involved. Instead, you'll be concentrating on the issues.

## Key points to remember

➤ If the buyer gets upset with you, focus on the issues, not personality.

➤ Calmly think to yourself, "Why is he doing this to me," and "What will it take to get him to stop?"

➤ Concentrate on the dollar amount that's being negotiated. Because the buyer seems angry with you, it may seem like a bigger deal than it really is.

➤ Remember Warren Christopher's admonition, "It's okay to get upset when you're negotiating, as long as you're in control and you're doing it as a specific negotiating tactic." It's when you're upset and out of control that you always lose.

➤ The only thing that matters is, "Where are we now, compared to where we were an hour ago, or yesterday or last week?"

# Chapter 10

# The Vise Gambit

The last of the Beginning Sales Negotiating Gambits I call the **Vise**, which is the simple little expression, "You'll have to do better than that." Here's how Power Sales Negotiators use it: The buyer has listened to your proposal and your pricing structure. You ignored his insistence that he's happy with his present supplier and you did a good job of building desire for your product. Finally, the buyer says to you, "I'm really happy with our present vendor, but I guess it wouldn't do any harm to have a backup supplier to keep them on their toes. I'll take one carload if you can get the price down to $1.22 per pound."

You respond with the Vise. You calmly say, "I'm sorry, you'll have to do better than that."

An experienced buyer will automatically respond with the Counter Gambit, which is, "Exactly how much better than that do I have to do?" In that way, he tries to pin you down to a specific. However, it will amaze you how often inexperienced buyers will concede a big chunk of their negotiating range simply because you did that.

Once you've said, "You'll have to do better than that," what's the next thing that you should do?

You've got it. Shut Up! Don't say another word. The buyer may just make a concession to you. Sales trainers call this the silent close, don't they? I'm sure that somebody taught you the silent close the first week that you were in the business. You make your proposal and then shut up. The buyer may just say yes, so it's foolish to say a word until you find out if he or she will accept your proposal.

I once watched two salespeople do the silent close on each other. There were three of us sitting at a circular conference table. The salesperson on my right wanted to buy a piece of real estate from the salesperson on my left. He made his proposal and then shut up, just as they taught him in sales training school. The more experienced salesperson on my left must have thought, "Son of a gun! I can't believe this! He's going to try the silent close on me? I'll teach him a thing or two. I won't talk either."

So, then I was faced with two strong-willed people who were both sitting there, daring the other to be the next one to talk. I didn't know how this was ever going to get resolved. There was dead silence in the room, except for the grandfather clock ticking away in the background. Obviously, they both knew what was going on, and neither one was willing to give in to the other. I didn't know how they would ever resolve this.

It seemed as though half an hour went by, although it was probably more like five minutes because silence seems like such a long time. Finally, the more experienced salesperson broke the impasse by scrawling the word "DECIZION?" on a pad of paper and sliding it across to the other salesperson. However, he had deliberately misspelled the word "decision," using a Z instead of an S. The younger salesperson looked at it and without thinking said, "You misspelled *decision.*" Then, once he started talking, he couldn't stop. (Do you know a salesperson like that? Once they start talking, they can't stop?) He went on to say, "If you're not willing to accept what I offered you, I might be willing to come up another $2,000. But not a penny more." He renegotiated his own proposal before he found out if the other person would accept it or not!

So, to use the Vise technique, Power Sales Negotiators simply response to the other side's proposal or counter-proposal with, "I'm sorry, you'll have to do better than that." And then shut up!

A client of mine called me up after a Secrets of Power Negotiating seminar that I had conducted for his managers and told me, "Roger, I thought you might like to know that we just made $14,000 using one of the Gambits that you taught us. We are having new equipment put into our Miami office. Our standard procedure has been to get bids from three qualified vendors and then take the lowest bid. So, I was sitting here going over the bids and was just about to okay the one I'd decided to accept. Then I remembered what you taught me about the Vise technique. So, I thought, 'What have I got to lose?' and scrawled across it, 'You'll have to do better than this,' and mailed it back to them. Their counter proposal came back $14,000 less than the proposal that I would have accepted."

You may be thinking, "Roger, you didn't tell me whether that was a $50,000 proposal, in which case it would have been a huge concession, or a multimillion dollar proposal, in which case it wouldn't have been that big a deal." Don't fall into the trap of negotiating percentages, when you should be negotiating dollars. The point was that he made $14,000 in the two minutes that it took him to scrawl that counter proposal across the bid. This meant that while he was doing it, he was generating $420,000 per hour of bottom-line profits. That's pretty good money, isn't it?

If you make a $2,000 concession to a buyer, it doesn't matter if you made it to get a $10,000 sale or a million-dollar sale. It's still $2,000 that you gave away. So, it doesn't make any sense for you to come back to your sales manager and say, "I had to make a $2,000 concession, but it's a $100,000 sale." What you should have been thinking was, "There is $2,000 sitting in the middle of the negotiating table. How much more time should I be willing to spend to see how much of it I could get?"

Have a feel for what your time is worth. Don't spend half an hour negotiating a $10 item (unless you're doing it just for the practice). Even if you got them to concede all of the $10, you'd only be making money at the rate of $20 an hour for the half-hour you invested in the negotiation. To put this in perspective for you, if you make $100,000 a year, you're making about $50 an hour. So, you should be thinking to yourself, "Is what I'm doing right now generating more than $50 per hour?"

Here's the point. When you have a deal in front of you that you could sell to your sales manager, but you're wondering if you could hang in a little bit longer and do a little bit better, you're not making $50 an hour. No, sir! You're making $50 a minute, and probably $50 a second!

And if that's not enough, remember that a negotiated dollar is a bottom-line dollar. It's not a gross sales dollar. So, the $2,000 that you may have conceded in seconds because you thought you needed to, to make the sale, is worth many times that in gross sales dollars. I've trained executives at discount retailers and health maintenance organizations (HMOs) where the profit margin is only 2 percent. They do a billion dollars worth of business a year, but they only bring in 2 percent in bottom-line profits. So, at their company, a $2,000 concession at the negotiating table has the same impact on the bottom-line as getting a $100,000 sale.

You're probably in an industry that does better than that. I have trained people at some companies where the bottom line is an incredible 25 percent of the gross sales. But that's the exception. In this country, the average profit margin is 5 percent of gross sales. So, probably that $2,000 concession you made is the equivalent of making a $40,000 sale. So, let me ask you something: How long would you be willing to work to get a $40,000 sale? An hour? Two hours? All day? I've had many sales managers tell me, "For a $40,000 sale I expect my sales people to work as long as it takes!" However fast-paced your business, you're probably willing to spend several hours to make a $40,000 sale. So, why are you so willing to make a $2,000 concession at the negotiating table? It has the same impact on the bottom-line as a $40,000 sale if your business generates the typical 5 percent bottom-line profit.

A negotiated dollar is a bottom-line dollar. I don't care if you do brain surgery in your spare time. You'll never make money faster than you will when you're negotiating!

Power Sales Negotiators always respond to a proposal with, "You'll have to do better than that."

**The Counter Gambit.** When the buyer uses the Vise on you, automatically respond with, "Exactly how much better than that do I have to do?" This is an attempt to get the buyer pinned down to a position. You should never make a concession to a buyer unless it's in response to a specific counter-proposal from them.

## Key points to remember

➤ Respond to a proposal or counter proposal with the Vise Gambit, "You'll have to do better than that."

➤ If it's used on you, respond with the Counter Gambit, "Exactly how much better than that do I have to do?" This will pin the buyer down to a specific.

➤ Concentrate on the dollar amount that's being negotiated. Don't be distracted by the gross amount of the sale and start thinking percentages.

➤ A negotiated dollar is a bottom-line dollar. Be aware of what your time is worth on an hourly basis.

➤ You'll never make money faster than you will when you're Power Sales Negotiating!

So, now I've taught you the Beginning Gambits of Power Sales Negotiating. The things that you do in the early stages of the negotiation to set it up for a successful win-win conclusion. In the next section, I'll move on to the Middle Sales Negotiating Gambits.

# Section Three

# Middle Sales Negotiating Gambits

# Chapter 11

# Higher Authority

You probably get very frustrated by the buyer who claims that he or she has to go to a **Higher Authority** before making a final decision. Unless you realize that this is simply a negotiating tactic that's being used on you, you feel that you'll never get to talk to the real decision-maker.

When I was president of a real estate company in California I used to have salespeople coming in to sell me things all the time: advertising, photocopy machines, computer equipment, and so on. I would always negotiate the very lowest price that I could, using all of these Gambits. Then I would say to them, "This looks fine. I do just have to run it by my board of directors, but I'll get back to you tomorrow with the final okay."

The next day I could get back to them and say, "Wow, are they tough to deal with right now. I felt sure I could sell it to them, but they just won't go along with it unless you can shave another couple of hundred dollars off the price." And I would get it. I didn't really need the board of directors to approve it and it never occurred to me that this deception was underhanded. I, and the buyers with whom you deal, see it as well within the rules by which one plays the game of negotiating.

So, when buyers say to you that they have to take it to the committee, that may not be true, but it's an effective negotiating tactic for them to use. So, let's first look at why you should use this Gambit and then I'll tell you how to handle it when the buyer uses it on you.

You would think that if you were going out to negotiate something, that you would want to have the authority to make a decision. At first glance it would seem that you would have more power if you were able to say to the buyer, "I have the power to make a deal with you."

So, you have a tendency to say to your sales manager, "Let me handle this. Give me the authority to cut the best possible deal."

Power Sales Negotiators know that you put yourself in a weakened negotiating position when you do that. You should always have to check with a Higher Authority before you can change your proposal or make a decision. Negotiators who present themselves as the decision-makers put themselves at a severe bargaining disadvantage. You have to put your ego on the back burner to do this, but you'll find it very effective.

The reason this works so well is simple: When buyers know that you have the final authority to make a deal, they know that they only have to convince *you*. If you're the final authority they don't have to work as hard to give you the benefits of the proposal because once you've given your approval, they know that they have consummated the deal.

Not so if you are telling them that you have to answer to a higher authority. When you have to get approval from region, head office, management, partners, or board of directors, buyers have to do more to convince you. They must make a proposal that you can take to your higher authority and get approved. Also, they know that they must completely win you over so that you'll want to persuade your higher authority to agree to the proposal.

Higher Authority works much better for you when your higher authority is a vague entity such as a committee or a board of directors. For example: Have you ever actually met a loan committee at a bank? I haven't. Bankers at my seminars have consistently told me that for loans of $500,000 or less, somebody at that bank can make a decision without having to go to loan committee. However, the loan officer knows that if he or she said to you, "Your package is on the president's desk," you would say, "Well, let's go talk to the president right now. Let's get it resolved." But you can't do that with the vague entity.

So, if you use the Higher Authority Gambit, be sure that your higher authority is a vague entity, such as a marketing committee or the people back at your head office. If you tell the buyer that your sales manager would have to approve it, what's the first thought that the buyer is going to have? Right! "Then why am I wasting time talking to you? If your sales manager is the only one who can make a decision, get your sales manager down here." However, when your higher authority is a vague, collective entity, they appear to be unapproachable. In all the years that I told salespeople that I had to run it by my board of directors, I only once had a salesperson say to me, "When does your board of directors meet? When can I make a presentation to them?"

At this point you may be thinking, "Roger, I can't use this. I own a small company that distributes electrical equipment, and everybody knows that I own it. They know that I don't have anybody above me with whom I have to check."

Sure you can use it. I own my own company, too, but there are decisions that I won't make unless I've checked with the people to whom I've delegated that area of responsibility.

If somebody asks me about doing a seminar for their company, I'll say, "Sounds good to me, but I have to check with my marketing people first, fair enough?" So, if you own your own company, your higher authority becomes the people in your organization to whom you've delegated authority.

Now that you've seen how much power you get by using Higher Authority, let's look at the benefits to buyers who use it against you:

1. They can put pressure on you without confrontation by saying, "We'd be wasting our time taking a proposal that high to the committee."

2. It unbalances you as a negotiator because it is so frustrating to feel that you're not able to present to the real decision-maker.

3. By inventing a higher authority, they can set aside the pressure of making a decision. When I was a real estate broker I would teach our agents that before they put buyers in their car to show them property, they should say to them, "Just to be sure I understand, if we find exactly the right home for you today, is there any reason why you wouldn't make a decision today?" The buyers may have interpreted this as putting pressure on them to decide quickly. But in fact it was simply eliminating their right to delay the decision by inventing a higher authority. If the agent didn't do this, they would very often defer the decision by saying, "We can't decide today because Uncle Harry is helping us with the down payment and we have to run it by him."

4. It sets them up for using the Vise technique: "You'll have to do better than that if you want to get it past committee."

5. It puts you in the position of needing the buyer to be on your side if it's to be approved by the committee.

6. They can make suggestions to you without implying that it's something to which they'd agree: "If you can come down another 10 percent, you may have a chance of the committee approving it."

7. It can be used to force you into a bidding war: "The committee has asked me to get five bids, and it looks as though they're going to take the lowest one."

8. The buyer can squeeze your price without revealing what you're up against: "The committee is meeting tomorrow to make a final decision. I know they've already gotten some really low bids, so there may not be any point in you submitting, but there's always a chance if you can come in with a super low proposal."

9. It sets the buyer up to use Good Guy/Bad Guy: "If it were up to me, I'd love to keep doing business with you, but the bean counters on the committee care only about the lowest price."

**The Counter Gambit.** You can see why buyers love to use the Higher Authority Gambit on you. Fortunately, Power Sales Negotiators know how to handle this challenge smoothly and effectively. Let me give you the Counter Gambits to Higher Authority:

***Make the first move.*** Your first approach should be to try to remove the buyer's resort to higher authority before the negotiations even start by getting them to admit that they could make a decision if the proposal was irresistible. This is exactly the same thing that I taught my real estate agents to say to the buyer before putting them in the car: "Let me be sure I understand; if we find exactly the right property for you today, is there any reason why you wouldn't make a decision today?" It's exactly the same thing that the car dealer will do to you when, before he lets you take it for a test drive, he says, "Let me be sure I understand; if you like this car as much as I know you're going to like it, is there any reason why you wouldn't make a decision today?" Because they know that if they don't remove your resort to Higher Authority up front, then there's a danger that under the pressure of asking for a decision, you will invent a Higher Authority as a delaying tactic.

So, before you present your proposal to the buyer, before you even get it out of your briefcase, you should casually say, "I don't mean to put any pressure on you..." (this, in terms of hidden meanings in conversation, is called a preparer—you've just prepared them for pressure. You've just given yourself permission to put pressure on them.) "I don't mean to put any pressure on you, but if we're going to go ahead on this we need to get it going right away. So let me ask you this: If this proposal meets all of your needs..." (That's as broad as any statement can be, isn't it?) "If this proposal meets all of your needs, is there any reason why you wouldn't give me a decision today?"

It's a harmless thing for the other person to agree to, because the other side is thinking, "If it meets all of my needs? No problem, there's loads of wriggle room there." However, if you can get them to respond with, "Well, sure if it meets all of my needs, I'll give you an okay right now," look at what you've accomplished:

1. You've eliminated their right to tell you that they want to want to think it over. If they say that, you say, "Well, let me go over it one more time. There must be something I didn't cover clearly enough because you did indicate to me earlier that you were willing to make a decision today."

2. You've eliminated their right to refer it to a Higher Authority. You've eliminated their right to say, "I want our specifications department (or the purchasing committee) to take a look at it."

***Don't give up.*** What if you're not able to remove their resort to Higher Authority? I'm sure there are many situations where you'll say that to a buyer, and they'll come right out and say, "I'm sorry but, on a purchase of this size, everything has to get approved by the specifications committee. I'll have to refer it to them for a final decision."

Here are the three steps that Power Sales Negotiators take when they're not able to remove the buyer's resort to Higher Authority:

**Step number one: Appeal to their ego.** With a smile on your face say, "But they always follow your recommendations, don't they?" With some personality styles, that's such an appeal to their ego that they'll say, "Well, I guess you're right. If I like it, then you can count on it." But more often than not, they'll say, "Well, yes, they usually follow my recommendations, but I can't give you a decision until I've taken it to the committee."

If you realize that you're dealing with egotistical buyers, try pre-empting their resort to Higher Authority early in your presentation by saying, "Do you think that if you took this to your supervisor, he'd approve it?" Often an ego-driven buyer will make the mistake of proudly telling you that they don't have to get anyone's approval.

**Step number two: Get a commitment that they'll take it to the committee with a positive recommendation.** You say, "But you will recommend it to them—won't you?" Hopefully they'll reply, "Yes, it looks like a good proposal to me, I'll go to bat for you with them."

In step two, Power Sales Negotiators get the buyers' commitment that they will go to the higher authority with a positive recommendation. There are only two things that can happen now. Either they'll say, yes, they will recommend it, or they'll say, no, they won't—because... Either way you've won. Their endorsement would be preferable, of course, but any time you can draw out an objection you should say, "Hallelujah." Because objections are buying signals. Buyers are not going to object to your price unless they are interested in buying from you. If they're not interested in buying from you, they don't care how much you're charging.

For a while I dated a woman whose hobby was interior decorating. One day she was all excited and dragged me down to the Orange County Design Center to show me a couch covered in kidskin. The leather was as soft and as supple as anything I'd ever felt. As I sat there, she said, "Isn't that a wonderful couch?"

I said, "No question about it, this is a wonderful couch."

She said, "And it's only $12,000."

I said, "Isn't that amazing? How can they do it for only $12,000?"

She said, "You don't have a problem with the price?"

I told her, "I don't have a problem with the price at all!"

Why didn't I have a problem with the price? Right! Because I had absolutely no intention of paying $12,000 for a couch, I don't care what they covered it with. Let me ask you this: If buying the couch interested me, would I have a problem with the price? Oh, you had better believe I'd have a problem with the price!

Objections are buying signals. We knew in real estate that if we were showing property and the people were "oohing" and "aaahing" all over the place, if they loved everything about the property, they weren't going to buy. The serious buyers were the ones who were saying, "Well the kitchen's not as big as we'd like. Hate that wallpaper. We'd probably end up knocking out that wall." Those people would buy.

Think about it. Have you ever in your life made a big sale, where the buyer loved your price up front? Of course not. All serious buyers complain about the price.

Your biggest problem is not an objection—it's indifference. I would rather they said to you, "I wouldn't buy widgets from your company if you were the last widget vendor in the world, because..." Than have them say to you, "I've been using the same source on widgets for 10 years, and he does fine. I don't want to take time to talk about making a change." Indifference is your problem, not objections.

Let me prove this to you. Give me the opposite of a word. If I say day, you say night. If I say black, you say white. Do you have the idea? Here's the question, "What is the opposite of love? If you said hate, think again. As long as they're throwing plates at you, you have something there you can work with! It's indifference that's the opposite of love. When they're saying to you, like Rhett Butler in *Gone with the Wind*, "Quite frankly, my dear, I don't give a damn!" That's when you know the movie is about over! Indifference is your problem, not objections. Objections are buying signals.

So, when you say to them, "You will recommend it to them, won't you?" they can either say, yes they will, or no they won't. Either way, you've won. Then you can move to Step Three.

**Step number three: The qualified *subject to* close.** The *subject to* close is a close that I'll teach you later in Section Six. It works because it turns a big decision into a little decision. The qualified *subject to* close in this instance would be, "Let's just write up the paper work *subject to* the right of your specifications committee to reject the proposal within a 24-hour period for any specifications reason." Or, "Let's just write up the paper work *subject to* the right of your legal department to reject the proposal within a 24-hour period for any legal reason."

Notice that you're not saying subject to their acceptance. That's too broad. You're saying *subject to* their right to decline it for a specific reason. If they're going to refer it to an attorney, it would be a legal reason. If they're going to refer it to their CPA, it would be a tax reason, and so on. Try to get it nailed down to a specific reason.

To recap, the three steps to take in response to a counter gambit if you're not able to get the buyer to waive his or her resort to Higher Authority:

1. Appeal to the buyer's ego.
2. Get the buyer's commitment that he'll recommend it to the higher authority.
3. The qualified *subject to* close.

***When the tables are turned.*** What if someone is trying to remove your Resort to Higher Authority? Let's say that a buyer is pressuring you to commit to price and terms on a shipment, but wants a decision right now. She's saying, "Harry, I love you like a brother, but I'm running a business not a religion. Give me what I need on this one right now, or I'll have to go with your competitor."

How do you handle it? Very simple. You say, "Jane, I'm happy to give you a decision. In fact, I'll give you an answer right now if you want it. But I have to tell you—if you force me to a decision now, the answer has to be no. Tomorrow, after I've had a chance to talk to my people, the answer might be yes. So, why don't you wait until tomorrow, and see what happens, fair enough?"

***Beware of escalating authority.*** You may find yourself in a situation where escalating authority is being used on you. You think that you have cut a deal, only to find that the head buyer has to approve it and won't. So, you sweeten the deal only to find that now the vice-president won't give approval. Escalating authority is, in my mind, outrageously unethical, but you do run into it. I'm sure that you've experienced it when trying to buy a car. After some preliminary negotiation, the salesperson surprises you by immediately accepting your low offer. After getting you to commit to a price (which sets you up psychologically to accept the idea that you will buy that car), the salesperson will say something like, "Well, this looks good. All I have to do is run this by my manager and the car is yours."

You can feel the car keys and ownership certificate in your hands already, and you're sitting there in the closing room congratulating yourself on getting such a good deal, when the salesperson returns with the sales manager. The manager sits down and reviews the price with you. He says, "You know, Fred was a little out of line here." Fred looks properly embarrassed. "This price is almost $500 under our factory invoice cost." He produces an official-looking factory invoice. "Of course, you can't possibly ask us to take a loss on the sale, can you?"

Now you feel embarrassed yourself. You're not sure how to respond. You thought you had a deal and Fred's higher authority just shot it down. Unaware that the dealer could sell you the car for 5 percent under invoice and still make money because of factory incentives, you fall for the sales manager's appeal to your sense of decency and nudge your offer up by $200. Again, you think you've bought the car, until the sales manager explains that at this incredibly low price, he needs to get his manager's approval. And so it goes. You find yourself working your way through a battalion of managers, each one able to get you to raise your offer by a small amount.

As a salesperson, being able to use and handle resort to Higher Authority is very critical to you when you're Power Sales Negotiating. Always maintain your own resort to Higher Authority. Always try to remove the buyer's resort to a Higher Authority.

**The Counter Gambits to use**, when you find the buyer using escalating authority on you, are these:

1. You can play this game also, by bringing in your own escalating levels of authority. The other side will quickly catch on to what you're doing, and call a truce.

2. At each escalating level of authority, you should go back to your opening negotiating position. Don't let them salami close you by letting each level of authority cut off another slice of your markup.

3. Don't think of it as a sale until you have final approval and the ink is dry on the contract. If you start mentally spending your commission, you'll be too emotionally involved in the sale to walk away.

4. Above all, don't get so frustrated that you lose your temper and walk away from what could be a profitable transaction for everybody. Sure, the tactic is unfair and unethical, but this is a business, not a religion, right? You're there to grease the wheels of commerce, not to convert the sinners.

# Key points to remember

➢ Don't let the buyer know that you have the authority to make a decision.

➢ Your higher authority should be a vague entity, not an individual.

➢ Even if you own your company you can still use this by referring down through your organization.

➢ Leave your ego at home when you're negotiating. Don't let the buyer trick you into admitting that you have authority.

➢ Attempt to get buyers to admit that they could approve your proposal if it meets all of their needs. If that fails, go through the three counter gambits:

1. Appeal to their ego.
2. Get their commitment that they'll recommend to their higher authority.
3. Go to a qualified *subject to* close.

➢ If they are forcing you to make a decision before you're ready to do so, offer to decide but let them know that the answer will be no, unless they give you time to check with your people.

➢ If they're using escalating authority on you, revert to your opening position at each level and introduce your own levels of escalating authority.

In this chapter, I've explained the use of the Higher Authority as a negotiating tactic. You should now also feel much more confident about handling the buyer who uses this tactic on you. In the next chapter, I'll teach you more of the Middle Sales Negotiating Gambits.

# Chapter 12

# Avoid Confrontational Negotiating

As you proceed into the middle stages of the negotiation and the issues become more defined, it's important that you **Avoid Confrontational Negotiation.** At this point, the buyer quickly gets a feel for whether you're working for a win-win solution, or whether you're a tough negotiator who's out for everything you can get.

That's one of the problems that I have with the way some attorneys negotiate—they can be very confrontational negotiators. You get that white envelope in the mail with black raised lettering in the top left-hand corner, and you think, "Oh no! What is it this time?" You open the letter and what's the first communication from the other side? It's a threat. What they're going to do with you if you don't give them what they want. But if they wanted to settle the case without expensive litigation (and I sometimes doubt their motives on that score) then they should never be confrontational in the early stages of the negotiation.

So, be very careful what you say at the beginning. If the buyer takes a position with which you totally disagree, don't argue! Arguing always intensifies the buyer's desire to prove himself or herself right. It's better to agree with the buyer initially and then turn it around using the Feel, Felt, Found formula. Respond with, "I understand exactly how you *feel* about that. Many other buyers have *felt* exactly the same way as you do right now. (Now you have diffused that competitive spirit. You're not arguing with him, you're agreeing with him.) But you know what we have always *found*? When we take a closer look at it with buyers, they have always found that..."

Let's look at some examples.

---

> The buyer says, "Your price is far too high." If you argue with him, he has a personal stake in proving you wrong and himself right. Instead, you say, "I understand exactly how you feel about that. Many other buyers have felt exactly the same way as you do when they first look at our program. However, when they take a closer look at what we offer, they have always found that we offer the best value in the marketplace."

> If the buyer says, "I hear that you people have problems in your shipping department," arguing with him will make him doubt your objectivity. Instead, say, "I understand how you could have heard that because I've heard it too. I think that rumor may have started a few years ago when we relocated our warehouse, but now major companies such as General Motors and General Electric trust us with their just-in-time inventories and we never have a problem."

> Let's say that the buyer tells you, "I don't believe in buying from off-shore suppliers. I think we should keep the jobs in this country." The more you argue, the more you'll force him into defending his position. Instead, say, "I understand exactly how you feel about that because these days many other people feel exactly the same way you do, but do you know what we have found? Since we have been having the initial assembly done in Thailand, we have actually been able to increase our American work force by more than 42 percent, and this is why...."

Instead of arguing up front, which creates confrontational negotiation, get in the habit of agreeing and then turning it around. Winston Churchill knew this. He was a grand old man, but he had one big weakness—he loved to drink. He was always battling with Lady Astor, who favored prohibition. One day she came up to him and said, "Winston, you are disgusting. You are drunk!" He was a good enough negotiator to know that you shouldn't argue. You should agree and then turn it around. He said, "Lady Astor, you're absolutely right; I am drunk. But you're ugly. And in the morning, I shall be sober."

When you argue, people argue back—it's instinct. At my seminars, I sometimes ask a person in the front row to stand. As I hold my two hands out with my palms facing toward the person, I ask her to place her hands against mine. Then, without saying another word, I gently start to push against the other person. Automatically, without any instruction, she begins to push back. People shove when you shove them. Similarly, when you argue with someone, it automatically makes him or her want to argue back.

The other great thing about Feel, Felt, Found is that it gives you time to think. Perhaps you're in a bar and this woman is saying to you, "I wouldn't let you buy me a drink if you were the last man in the world!" You haven't heard anything like this before. It shocks you. You don't know what to say. But if you have Feel, Felt, Found in the back of your mind, you can say, "I understand exactly how you feel about that. Many other people have felt exactly the same way. However, I have always found..."

And by the time you get there, you'll have thought of something to say. Similarly, you sometimes catch buyers at a bad moment. You may call to get an appointment and when you arrive the buyer says, "I don't have time to waste talking to some lying scum-sucking salesperson!" You calmly say, "I understand exactly how you feel about that. Many other people have felt exactly the same way. However..." And by the time you get there you'll have recovered your composure and will know exactly what to say!

**The Counter Gambit.** When a buyer uses Feel, Felt, Found on you, acknowledge the objection but go to the Vise Gambit: "I hear what you're saying, but we can't make even the slimmest of profits at the price you're suggesting. You'll just have to do better than that."

# Key points to remember

➤ Don't argue with the buyer if he disputes what you say because it creates confrontation.

➤ Use the Feel, Felt, Found formula to turn the hostility around.

➤ Having Feel, Felt, Found in the back of your mind gives you time to think when the buyer throws some unexpected hostility your way.

# Chapter 13

# The Declining Value of Services

Now let me tell you about the principle of the **Declining Value of Services**. It teaches you something that you can count on in dealing with buyers: Any concession you make to them will quickly lose its value. The value of any material object you buy may go up in value over the years, but the value of services always appears to decline rapidly after you have performed those services.

For this reason Power Sales Negotiators know that any time you make a concession to the buyer in a negotiation, you should ask for a reciprocal concession right away because the favor that you did the buyer now loses value very quickly. Two hours from now the value of it will have diminished substantially.

Real estate salespeople are very familiar with the principle of the Declining Value of Services. When a seller of a property has a problem with it, and the real estate salesperson offers to solve that problem for a 6-percent listing fee, it doesn't sound like an enormous amount of money. However, the minute that she has performed the service by finding the buyer, then suddenly that 6 percent starts to sound like a tremendous amount of money. "Six percent! That's $12,000!" the seller is saying. "For what? What did she do? All she did was put it in a multiple listing service." They did much more than that to market the property and negotiate the contract, but remember the principle: The value of a service always appears to diminish rapidly after you have performed that service.

I'm sure you've experienced that, haven't you? Buyers with whom you do a small amount of business call you. They're in a state of panic because the supplier from whom they get the bulk of their business has let them down on a shipment. Now their entire assembly line has to shut down tomorrow unless you can work miracles and get a shipment to them first thing in the morning. Sound familiar? So, you work all day and through the night, rescheduling shipments all over the place. Against all odds, you're able to get a shipment there just in time for the assembly line to keep operating. You even show up at the buyer's plant and personally supervise the unloading of the shipment. And the buyer loves you for it! He or she comes down to the dock, where you are triumphantly wiping the dirt off your hands, and says, "I can't believe you were able to do that for me. That is unbelievable service! You are incredible! Love you, love you, love you."

So, you say, "Happy to do it for you, Joe. That's the kind of service we can give when we have to. Don't you think it's time you considered my company as your sole supplier?"

He replies, "That does sound good, but I don't have time to talk about it now because I've got to get over to the assembly line and be sure that it's running smoothly. Come to my office Monday morning at 10 o'clock, and we'll go over it. Better yet, come by at noon and I'll buy you lunch. I really appreciate what you did for me. You are fantastic. Love you, love you, love you."

So, all weekend long, you think to yourself, "Boy! Do I have this one made! Does he owe me!" However, Monday rolls around and negotiating with the buyer is just as hard as ever. What went wrong? The Declining Value of Services came into play. The value of a service always appears to decline rapidly after you have performed the service.

It tells you that if you make a concession during a negotiation, get a reciprocal concession right away. Don't wait. Don't be sitting there thinking that because you did them a favor, they owe you, and that they will make it up to you later. With all the goodwill in the world, the value of what you did goes down rapidly.

Plumbers know this principle, don't they? They know that the time to negotiate with you is before they do the work, not after. I had a plumber out to the house. After looking at the problem, he slowly shook his head and said, "Mr. Dawson, I know what the problem is, and I can fix it for you. It will cost you $150."

I said, "Fine, go ahead."

You know how long it took him to do the work? Five minutes! I said, "Now wait a minute. You're going to charge me $150 for five minutes' work? I'm a nationally known speaker, and I don't make that kind of money!"

IIe replied, "I didn't make that kind of money either—when I was a nationally known speaker!"

**The Counter Gambit.** If you sell a service, remember that the value of that service will go down quickly once it has been performed. Agree on the price before you start the work. Agree on a formula to use if circumstances change and you need to increase the fee. Get paid in advance if you can. If you can't get paid in advance, get paid incrementally as the work is being done, or as quickly as possible after the work is done.

## Key points to remember

➢ The value of a material object may go up, but the value of services always appears to go down.
➢ Don't make a concession and trust that the other side will make it up to you later.
➢ Negotiate your fee before you do the work.

## Chapter 14

# Never Offer to Split the Difference

The next rule is that you should **Never Offer to Split the Difference** when you're negotiating. In this country, we have a tremendous sense of fair play. Our sense of fair play dictates to us that if both sides give equally, then that's fair. If Fred puts his home up for sale at $200,000 and Susan makes an offer at $190,000, and both Fred and Susan are eager to compromise, both of them tend to be thinking, "If we settled at $195,000 that would be fair because we both gave equally." Maybe it's fair, and maybe it isn't. It depends on the opening negotiating positions that Fred and Susan took. If the house is really worth $190,000 and Fred was only holding to his overinflated price to take advantage of Susan having falling in love with his house, then it's not fair. If the house is worth $200,000 and Susan is willing to pay that, but is taking advantage of Fred's financial problems, then it isn't fair. So, don't fall into the trap of thinking that splitting the difference is the fair thing to do when you can't resolve a difference in price with the buyer.

With that misconception out of the way, let me point out that Power Sales Negotiators know that splitting the difference does not mean splitting it down the middle. Just split the difference twice and the split becomes 75 percent/25 percent. Furthermore, you may be able to get the other party to split the difference three or more times. I once negotiated with a bank that had a blanket encumbrance over several properties that I owned. I had sold one property out from under the blanket and our contract entitled them to a $32,000 pay-down of the loan. I offered them $28,000. I got them to offer to split the difference at $30,000. Over a period of weeks until the sale closed, I was able to get them to offer to split the difference again at $29,000, and at $28,500, and finally they agreed to $28,250.

Here's how that this Gambit works:

The first thing to remember is that you should never offer to split the difference yourself, but always encourage the other person to offer to split the difference.

Let's say that you're a salesperson for a building contractor. You have been working to get a remodeling job that you bid at $86,000 and where they offered $75,000. You've been negotiating for a while during which time you've been able to get the owners of the property up to $80,000, and you've come down to $84,000 with your proposal. Where do you go from there? You have a strong feeling that if you offered to split the difference they would agree to do so, which would mean agreeing at $82,000.

Instead of offering to split the difference, here's what you should do. You say, "Well, I guess this is just not going to fly. It seems like such a shame though, when we've both spent so much time working on this proposal." (People become more flexible in relationship to how long they've been negotiating.) "We've spent so much time on this proposal, and we've come so close to a price with which we could both live. It seems like a shame that it's all going to collapse when we're only $4,000 apart."

If you keep stressing the time that you've spent on it, and the small amount of money that you're apart on the price, eventually the other people will say, "Look, why don't we split the difference."

You act dumb and say, "Let's see, splitting the difference, what would that be? I'm at $84,000, and you're at $80,000. What you're telling me is you'd come up to $82,000? Is that what I hear you saying?"

"Well, yes," they say. "If you'll come down to $82,000, then we'll settle for that." In doing this you have immediately shifted the negotiating range from $80,000 to $82,000. The negotiating range is now $82,000 to $84,000 and you have yet to concede an additional dime.

So, you say, "$82,000 sounds a lot better than $80,000. Tell you what, let me talk to my partners, (or whatever other Higher Authority you've set up) and see how they feel about it. I'll tell them you came up to $82,000, and we'll see if we can't put it together now. I'll get back to you tomorrow."

The next day you get back to them and you say, "Wow, are my partners tough to deal with right now! I felt sure that I could get them to go along with $82,000 but we spent two hours last night going over the figures again, and they insist that we'll lose money if we go a penny below $84,000. But good golly! We're only $2,000 apart on this job now. Surely, we're not going to let it all fall apart when we're only $2,000 apart."

If you keep that up long enough, eventually they'll offer to split the difference again.

If you are able to get them to split the difference again, this Gambit has made you an extra $1,000 of bottom-line profit. However, even if you can't get them to split the difference again, and you end up at the same $82,000 that you would have done if *you* had offered to split the difference, something very significant has happened here. What was the significant thing that happened?

Right! They think they won because you got them to propose splitting the difference at $82,000. Then you got your partners to reluctantly agree to a proposal that they had made. If you had suggested splitting the difference, then you would have been putting a proposal on the table and forcing them to agree to a proposal that you had made.

That may seem like a very subtle thing to you, but it can dramatically affect who felt they won and who felt they lost. Remember that the essence of Power Sales Negotiating is to always leave the other side thinking that they won.

So, the rule is Never Offer to Split the Difference, but always encourage the other person to offer to split the difference.

**The Counter Gambit.** When the buyer tries to get you to split the difference, use Higher Authority and Good Guy/Bad Guy. "It sounds reasonable to me, but I don't have the authority. If you'll propose it I'll take it to my people and see if I can get them to accept it."

# Key points to remember

➢ Don't fall into the trap of thinking that splitting the difference is the fair thing to do.

➢ Splitting the difference doesn't mean down the middle, because you can do it more than once.

> ➤ Never offer to split the difference, but instead encourage the other side to offer to split the difference.

> ➤ By getting them to offer to split the difference, you put them in a position of suggesting the compromise. Then you can reluctantly agree to their proposal, making them feel that they won.

# Chapter 15

# The Hot Potato

The **Hot Potato** is when buyers want to give you their problem and have you make it your problem. It's like tossing you a Hot Potato at a barbecue.

What Hot Potatoes do your buyers toss you?

Do you ever hear, "We just don't have it in the budget"? Whose problem is it that they didn't budget properly for your fine product or service? It's their problem, right? Not yours. But they'd like to toss it to you and make it yours.

How about, "I can't authorize that"? Whose problem is it that she hasn't developed the trust of the people to whom she reports? It's hers, right? Not yours. But she'd like to toss it to you and make it yours.

You've probably had a customer call you to say, "I need you to move my delivery up. If those parts are not here first thing in the morning, the entire assembly line comes to a screeching halt." Whose scheduling problem is that? His, right? Not yours. But what he'd like to do is toss you his problem and make it yours.

I've found out from my study of international negotiations that exactly the same principles apply. The same rules that apply for the negotiators in Geneva during nuclear control talks apply to you when the other side is putting pressure on you. Here's how the international negotiators would tell you to respond to the Hot Potato: Test it for validity right away. This is what international negotiators do when the other side tries to give them their problem. You have to find out right away whether it really is a deal killer that they've tossed you or simply something they threw onto the negotiating table to judge your response. You must jump on it right away. Later is too late. If you continue to work on their problem, soon they believe that now it's your problem and it's too late to test it for validity.

My background is as a real estate broker. I used to be president of a 28-office company in Southern California. In real estate we used to get tossed the Hot Potato all the time. It was the buyer who would come into one of our offices and say, "We have only $10,000 to put down." Even in blue-collar areas, that would be a very low down payment. Our real estate agent could possibly work with it, but it would be tough.

I would teach the agents to test it for validity right away—to tell the buyers, "Maybe we can work with $10,000. But let me ask you this: If I find exactly the right property for you, in exactly the right neighborhood, the price and terms are fantastic, your family is going to love it, your kids are going to love having their friends over to play. But it takes $15,000 to get in—is there any point in showing it to you, or should I just show it to my other buyers?"

Once in a great while the person would respond, "Don't you speak English? Watch my lips, $10,000 is it and not a penny more. I don't care how good a buy it is." But nine times out of 10 they would say, "Well, we really didn't want to touch our Certificate of Deposit, but if it's a really good buy, we might. Or maybe Uncle Joe would help us with the down payment." Immediately the agent found out that the problem the buyers tossed her was not the deal killer that it had appeared to be.

If you sell home furnishings, one of your customers might say, "We've got $20 a square yard for carpeting and that's it." If you catch that Hot Potato instead of tossing it back you will probably start thinking of cutting prices right away because you assumed that what they told you was final.

But instead you test for validity up front by saying, "If I could show you a carpet that would give you double the wear and still look good five years from now, but cost only 10 percent more, you'd want to take a look at it, wouldn't you?" Nine times out of 10 they'll say, "Sure, we'll take a look at it," and immediately you know that the price issue is not the deal buster that it appeared to be.

Another way to counter the Hot Potato of "We don't have it in the budget" is to simply say, "Well, who has the authority to exceed the budget?" Sometime you'll kick yourself at what happens next. They'll say, "Well that would take a vice president to authorize that." So, you say, "Well you want to do it, don't you? Why don't you call the vice president and see if you can get an okay to exceed the budget, fair enough?" And he'll pick up the phone to call the vice president and argue for an okay. Sometimes, it's that simple. But you have to test for validity right away.

I remember doing a seminar for the Associated General Contractors of Alaska. They put me up at the Anchorage Hilton and on my departure day I needed a late checkout. There were two clerks standing right next to each other behind the registration desk and I said to one of them, "Would you give me a 6 o'clock checkout in my room, please."

She said, "Mr. Dawson, we could do that for you, but of course we'd have to charge you for an extra half-day."

I said, "Who would have the authority to waive that charge?"

She pointed to the person standing next to her and said, "She would." The person standing right next to her!

So I leaned over and said to the other person, "How would you feel about that?"

She said, "Oh, sure. That would be fine. Go ahead."

Another way to handle the *we don't have it in the budget* Hot Potato is to ask when the budget year ends. I trained 80 salespeople at one of the top HMOs in California. A few weeks before the meeting the training director called me and suggested that we have dinner together so that she could fill me in on how the company operates. Because I figured that she was going to pay for dinner I picked the top French restaurant in Orange County and we had a great dinner. As they were serving desert I said, "You know what you should do? You should invest in a set of my cassette tapes for each of your salespeople so that they have the advantage of a continuous learning process." As I said that I was mentally computing that 80 salespeople at $65 per set of tapes would be another $5,200 income on top of the speaking fee to which they'd already agreed.

She thought about it and said, "Roger, that probably would be a good idea, but we just don't have it in the budget."

I need to make a confession here. I'm very ashamed of what I thought next, but I want to share it with you because it may help you if you've ever had the same shameful thought. I thought, "I wonder if I cut the price she would say yes." Isn't that a shameful thought? She hadn't said a thing about the tapes costing too much. She hadn't told me that she might be tempted if I lowered my price. She had simply told me that she didn't have it in the budget.

Fortunately I caught myself in time and instead did what I teach, which is to test for validity. I asked, "When does your budget year end?" This was in August and I thought that she would tell me it ended December 31.

To my surprise she said, "At the end of September."

"So, you would have it in the budget on October 1?"

"Yes, I suppose that we would."

"Then, no problem. I'll ship you the tapes and bill you on October 1, fair enough?"

"That would be fine," she told me. In less than 30 seconds, I had made a $5,200 sale, because I knew that when she tossed me what was essentially her problem, I should test for validity.

I was feeling so good about this that when the waiter brought the bill I slid my American Express card into the leather case. He took it away and she quietly said, "Roger, we were thinking of paying for dinner." So, I thought, "Roger, there are days when nothing goes right. You suffer through those. This is a day when nothing can go wrong, so why not relish it?" So, I called the waiter back and told him that we gave him the wrong credit card!

So, look out for people giving you their problems. You have enough of your own, don't you? It's like the businessperson who was pacing the floor at night. He couldn't sleep and his wife was getting frantic. "Darling, what's bothering you? Why don't you come to bed?"

He said, "Well, we have this huge loan payment due tomorrow and the bank manager is a good friend of ours. I just hate to face him and say that we're not going to have the money to pay him."

So, his wife picked up the phone, called their friend the bank manager, and said, "That loan payment we have coming due tomorrow, we don't have the money to pay it."

The husband exploded. He said, "What did you do that for? That's what I was afraid of."

And she said, "Well, dear, now it's his problem and you can come to bed."

Don't let other people give you their problems.

**The Counter Gambit.** When someone hands you a Hot Potato, test for validity right away by asking, "Who has the authority to exceed the budget?" or "Who has the authority to waive that charge?" or "When does your budget year end?" If you can break through the barrier of the problem they're trying to give you, even if it is hypothetical, you have eliminated the Hot Potato.

## Key points to remember

➢ Don't let other people toss you their problems.

➢ When they do, test for validity right away. You must find out whether this really is a deal killer, or just something they threw out to see what your reaction would be.

➢ Don't buy into their procedural problems. A procedure is just something that somebody once wrote down. So somebody in their organization has the power to change the procedure or ignore it.

➢ Don't react to every problem by thinking that you have to lower your price. Price may not be the issue at all. Think to yourself, "How can I resolve this issue without having to give the buyer a better deal?"

# Chapter 16

# Trading Off

Now let's talk about the last of the Middle Sales Negotiating Gambits, **Trading Off**. The Trade Off Gambit tells you that any time the buyer asks you for a concession in the negotiations, you should automatically ask for something in return. The first time you use this Gambit, you'll get back the money you invested in this book many times over, and it will earn you thousands of dollars every year, from that point on.

Let's say that you sell forklifts and you've sold a large order to a warehouse, style hardware store. They've requested delivery on August 15, 30 days ahead of their grand opening. Then the operations manager for the chain calls you and says, "We're running ahead of schedule on the store construction. We're thinking of moving up the store opening to take in the Labor Day weekend. Is there any way you could move up delivery of those fork lifts to next Wednesday?" You may be thinking, "That's great. They're sitting in our local warehouse ready to go, so I'd much rather move up the shipment and get paid sooner. We'll deliver them tomorrow if you want them."

Although your initial inclination is to say, "That's fine," I still want you to use the Trade Off Gambit.

I want you to say, "Quite frankly I don't know whether we can get them there that soon. I'll have to check with my scheduling people," (note the use of a vague Higher Authority) "and see what they say about it, but let me ask you this, if we can do that for you, what can you do for us?"

One or all of three things is going to happen:

1. You might just get something. They may just have been thinking, "Boy have we got a problem here. What can we give them as an incentive to get them to move this shipment up?" So, they may just concede something to you. They may just say, "I'll tell accounting to cut the check for you today." Or "Take care of this for me, and I'll use you again for the store that we're opening in Chicago in December."

2. By asking for something in return, you've elevated the value of the concession. When you're negotiating, why give anything away? Always make a big deal out of it. You may need that later. Later you may need to be able to go to them and say, "Do you remember last August when you needed me to move that shipment up for you? You know how hard I had to talk to my people to get them to re-schedule all our shipments? We did that for you, so don't make me wait for our money. Cut me the check today, won't you?" When you elevate the value of the concession, you set it up for a trade off later.

3. It stops the grinding away process. This is the key reason why you should always use the Trade Off Gambit. If they know that every time they ask you for something, you're going to ask for something in return, then it stops them constantly coming back for more. I can't tell you how many times a salesperson has come up to me at a seminar or called my office and said, "Roger, can you help me with this? We thought we had a sweetheart of a deal put together. We didn't think that we would have any problems at all with this one; but in the very early stages, they asked us for a very small concession. We were so happy to have their business that we told me, 'Sure, we can do that.' A week later they called us for another small concession, and we said: 'All right, I guess we can do that, too.' Ever since then, it's been one darn thing after another. Now it looks as though the whole thing is going to fall apart on us." They should have known up front that when the other side asked them for that first small concession, they should have asked for something in return. "If we can do that for you, what can you do for us?"

I trained the top 50 salespeople at a Fortune 50 company that manufactures office equipment. They have a Key Account Division that negotiates their largest accounts with their biggest customers. These people are heavy hitters. There was a salesperson at the seminar who had just made a $43 million sale to an aircraft manufacturer. (That's not a record. When I trained people at a huge computer manufacturer's training headquarters, I had a salesperson in the audience who'd just closed a $3 billion sale. And he was in *my* seminar taking notes!)

This Key Account Division had its own vice president and he came up to me afterward to tell me, "Roger, that thing you told us about trading off was the most valuable lesson I've ever learned in any seminar. I've been coming to seminars like this for years, and thought that I'd heard it all, but I'd never been taught what a mistake it is to make a concession without asking for something in return. That's going to save us hundreds of thousands of dollars in the future."

Jack Wilson, who produced some video training tapes for me, told me that soon after I taught him this Gambit, he used it to save several thousand dollars. A television studio called him and told him that one of their camera operators was sick. Would Jack mind if they called a camera operator that Jack had under contract and ask him if he could fill in? It was just a courtesy call. Something that Jack would have said, "No problem," to in the past. However, this time he said, "If I do that for you, what will you do for me?" To his surprise, they said, "Tell you what. The next time you use our studio, if you run into overtime, we'll waive the overtime charge." They had just conceded several thousand dollars to Jack, on something that he never would have asked for in the past.

Please use these Gambits word for word the way I'm teaching them to you. If you change even a word, it can dramatically change the effect. If, for example, you change this from, "If we can do that for you what can you do for us?" to "If we do that for you, you will have to do this for us," you have become confrontational, and at a very sensitive point in the negotiations, when the other side is under pressure and is asking you for a favor. Of course, you're tempted to take advantage of this situation and ask for something specific in return. Don't do it. It could cause the negotiation to blow up in your face.

When you ask what they will give you in return, they may say, "Not a darn thing," or "You get to keep our business, that's what you get." That's fine, because you had everything to gain by asking, and you haven't lost anything.

If necessary, you can always revert to a position of insisting on a trade off by saying, "I don't think I can get my people to agree to that unless you're prepared to accept a charge for expedited shipping," or "Unless you're willing to move up the payment date."

**The Counter Gambit.** What should you do if the buyer uses this Gambit on you? Let's say that you have made a reasonable request of the buyer. Perhaps what you sell is in short supply and you're asking the buyer to take half the shipment now, and the other half in the week. You know that this is not a big inconvenience for the buyer, but he decides to take advantage of you by asking for something in return. Here are three possible responses:

> ➤ Ask him what he wants and give it to him if the request is reasonable. Remember what I told you in Chapter 9: Concentrate on the issues. Don't turn a small problem into a big one because you're upset that the buyer out-negotiated you.
> ➤ Tell him that you've already given him the best deal in the world. Blame your Higher Authority (see Chapter 11).
> ➤ Position the buyer for easy acceptance (see Chapter 21) by refusing his request but offering a token concession, just so that he feels he won something.

# Key points to remember

> ➤ When asked for a small concession by the other side, always ask for something in return.
> ➤ Use this expression, "If we can do that for you, what can you do for me?"
> ➤ You may just get something in return.
> ➤ It elevates the value of the concession so that you can use it as a trade-off later.
> ➤ Most important, it stops the grinding away process.
> ➤ Don't change the wording and ask for something specific in return because it's too confrontational.

So, now you've learned the Middle Sales Negotiating Gambits—the things you do to keep up the momentum of the negotiations. In the next chapter, I'll start to teach you the Ending Sales Negotiating Gambits— the things you do as you prepare to get the buyer's commitment.

# Section Four

# Ending Sales Negotiating Gambits

# Chapter 17

# Good Guy/Bad Guy

**Good Guy/Bad Guy** is one of the best known negotiating gambits. Charles Dickens first wrote about it in his book *Great Expectations*. In the opening scene of the story, the young hero Pip is in the graveyard when out of the sinister mist came a large, very frightened man. He is a convict, and he has chains around his legs. He asks Pip to go into the village and bring back food and a file, so he can remove the chains. The convict has a dilemma, however. He wants to scare the child into doing as he's asked, yet he mustn't put so much pressure on Pip that he'll freeze with fear or bolt into town to tell the police.

The solution to the convict's problem is to use the Good Guy/Bad Guy Gambit. I'm taking some liberty with the original work, but what the convict says in effect, is, "You know, Pip, I like you and I would never do anything to hurt you. But I have to tell you that waiting out here in the mist is a friend of mine, and he can be violent, and I'm the only one who can control him. If I don't get these chains off—if you don't help me get them off—then my friend might come after you. So, you have to help me. Do you understand?" Good Guy/Bad Guy is a very effective way of putting pressure on people, without confrontation.

I'm sure you've seen Good Guy/Bad Guy used in the old police movies. Officers bring a suspect into the police station for questioning, and the first detective to interrogate him is a rough, tough, mean looking person. He threatens the suspect with all kinds of things that they're going to do to him. Then he's mysteriously called away to take a phone call and the second detective, who's brought in to look after the prisoner while the first detective is away, is the warmest, nicest guy in the entire world. He sits down and makes friends with the prisoner. He gives him a cigarette and says, "Listen kid, it's really not as bad as all that. I've kind of taken a liking to you and I know the ropes around here. Why don't you let me see what I can do for you with them?" It's a real temptation to think that the Good Guy's on your side, when of course, he really isn't.

Then the Good Guy would go ahead and close on what you would recognize as a minor point close. "All I think the detectives really need to know," he tells the prisoner, "is where did you buy the gun?" What they really want to know is, "Where did you hide the body?"

Starting out with a minor point like that and then working up from there works very well, doesn't it? It's the car salesperson who says to you, "If you did invest in this car would you get the blue or the gray?" "Would you want the vinyl upholstery or the leather?" Little decisions lead up to big ones.

It's the real estate salesperson who says, "If you did invest in this home, how would you arrange the furniture in the living room?" Or, "Which of these bedrooms would be the nursery for your new baby?" The Good Guy asks for little decisions knowing it will build up to big decisions.

Buyers work Good Guy/Bad Guy on you much more than you might believe. Look out for it anytime you find yourself dealing with two people. Chances are you'll see it being used on you, in one form or another.

For example, you may sell corporate health insurance plans for an HMO and have an appointment to meet with the vice president of Human Resources at a company that manufactures lawn mowers. When the secretary leads you in to meet with the vice president, you find to your surprise that the president of the company wants to sit in and listen in on your presentation.

That's negotiating two on one, which is not good, but you go ahead and everything appears to be going along fine. So, you feel that you have a good chance of closing the sale, until the president suddenly starts getting irritated. Eventually he says to his vice president, "Look, I don't think these people are interested in making a serious proposal to us. I'm sorry, but I've got things to do." Then he storms out of the room.

This really shakes you up if you're not used to negotiating. Then the vice president says, "Wow! Sometimes he gets that way, but I really like the plan that you presented, and I think we can still work this out. If you could be a little more flexible on your price, then I think we can still put it together. Tell you what—why don't you let me see what I can do for you with him?"

If you don't realize what they're doing to you, you'll hear yourself say something like, "What do you think the president would agree to?" Then it won't be long before you'll have the vice president negotiating for you—and he or she is not even on your side!

If you think I'm exaggerating on this one, consider this: Haven't you, at one time or another, said to a car salesperson, "What do you think you could get your sales manager to agree to?" As if the salesperson is on your side and not on theirs? Haven't we all, when buying real estate, found the property we want to own and asked the agent who has helped us find it, "What do you think the sellers would take?" Let me ask you something. Who is your agent working for? Who is paying her? It's not you, is it? She is working for the seller and yet she has effectively played Good Guy/Bad Guy with us. So, look out for it because you run into it a lot.

When I was the president of a large real estate company in California, we had one branch that consistently lost money. The branch had been open about a year but we had signed a three-year lease on the premises, which committed us to try to make it work for two more years. However, no matter how hard I tried, I couldn't find a way to either increase the income or decrease the expenses of the office. The biggest problem was the lease. We were paying $1,700 a month, and that one expense was what was killing our profit.

I called the property owner and explained my problem and tried to get him to reduce the rent to $1,400 a month, a figure that would let us eke out a profit. He said, "You have two more years on that lease and you're just going to have to live with it." I used every other Gambit I knew, but nothing would budge him. It looked as though I would just have to accept the situation.

Finally, I tried the Good Guy/Bad Guy Gambit combined with a great deal of time pressure. Several weeks later I called him up at 5:50 in the evening. "About that lease," I said. "A problem has come up here. I want you to know that I really agree with your position. I signed a three-year lease and there are more than two years left on it, and there isn't any question that we should live with it, but here's the problem: I have to go into my board of directors meeting in half an hour and they're going to ask me if you've been willing to reduce the lease to $1,400. If I have to tell them no, they'll tell me to close the office."

"I'll sue!" protested the property owner.

"I know. I agree with you entirely," I said. "I'm squarely on your side, but the problem is the board of directors with whom I have to deal. If you threaten to sue, they'll just say, 'Okay, let him sue. This is Los Angeles County, and it will take him two years to get into court.'"

His response demonstrates how effective the Good Guy/Bad Guy Gambit can be. He said, "Would you go into that board meeting and see what you can do for me? I'd be willing to split the difference and reduce the lease to $1,550, but if they won't settle for that, I could drop it as low as $1,500." The Gambit had worked so well that he actually asked me to negotiate for him with my own board of directors!

See how effective it can be in putting pressure on the other side without confrontation? What would have happened if I had said to him, "Go ahead and sue me. It'll take you two years to get into court!"? It would have upset him so much that we would have spent the next two years talking to each other through attorneys. By using a vague higher authority as my bad guy, I was able to put incredible pressure on him without having him get upset with me.

This Gambit is still very effective even when everybody knows what's going on. It was how Presidents Carter and Reagan got the hostages out of Iran, wasn't it? You remember that? Carter had lost the election. He was very eager to do something about the Iranian hostage situation before he left the White House and Reagan could take credit for their release. So, he started playing Good Guy/Bad Guy with the Ayatollah. He said to him, "If I were you, I'd settle this thing with me. Don't take a chance on this new team coming into office in January. My goodness, have you taken a look at these guys? The president's a former cowboy actor. The vice president is the former head of the CIA; The Secretary of State is Alexander Haig. These guys are crazier than Englishmen. There's no telling what they might do."

Reagan, playing along with it, said, "Hey, if I were you, I'd settle with Carter. He's a nice guy. You're definitely not going to like what I'll have to say about it, when I get into the White House." Sure enough, we saw the hostages being released on the morning of Reagan's inauguration. Of course, the Iranians were aware of Good

Guy/Bad Guy, but they didn't want to take a chance that Reagan would follow through with his threats. It demonstrated that these Gambits work even when the other side knows what you're doing.

In fact, when you're Power Sales Negotiating with someone who understands all of these Gambits, it becomes more fun. It's like playing chess with a person of equal skill rather than someone whom you can easily outsmart.

**The Counter Gambits.** Try these Counter Gambits when someone pulls a Good Guy/Bad Guy on you:

1. The first Counter Gambit is simply to identify the Gambit. Although there are many other ways to handle the problem, this one is so effective that it's probably the only one you need to know. Good Guy/Bad Guy is so well-known that it embarrasses people when they get caught using it. When you notice the other side using it you should smile and say, "Oh, come on—you aren't going to play Good Guy/Bad Guy with me are you? Come on, sit down, let's work this thing out." Usually their embarrassment will cause them to retreat from the position.

2. You could respond by creating a Bad Guy of your own. Tell them that you'd love to do what they want, but the people back at the head office are obsessed with sticking to the program. You can always make a fictitious Bad Guy appear more unyielding than a Bad Guy who is present at the negotiation.

3. You could go over their heads to their supervisor. For example, if you're dealing with a buyer and head buyer at a distributorship, you might call the owner of the distributorship and say, "Your buyers were playing Good Guy/Bad Guy with me. You don't approve of that kind of thing, do you?" (Be careful about going over the buyer's head because the bad feelings it can cause may create some real problems for you.)

4. Sometimes just letting the bad guy talk resolves the problem, especially if he's being obnoxious. Eventually his own people will get tired of hearing it and tell him to knock it off!

5. You can counter Good Guy/Bad Guy by saying to the Good Guy, "Look, I understand what you two are doing to me. From now on anything that he says, I'm going to attribute to you also." So, now you have two bad guys to deal with, so it diffuses the Gambit. Sometimes just identifying them both in your own mind as bad guys will handle it, without you having to come out and accuse them.

6. If the other side shows up with an attorney or controller who is clearly there to play bad guy, jump right in and forestall their role. Say to them, "I'm sure you're here to play bad guy, but let's not take that approach. I'm as eager to find a solution to this situation as you are, so why don't we all take a win-win approach. Fair enough?" This really takes the wind out of their sails!

## Key points to remember

➢ Buyers use Good Guy/Bad Guy on you much more than you might believe. Look out for it whenever you're negotiating with two or more people.

➢ It is a very effective way of putting pressure on the other person without creating confrontation.

➢ Counter it by identifying it. It's such a well-known tactic that when you catch them using it, they get embarrassed and back off.

## Chapter 18

# Nibbling

Now let's talk about **Nibbling**. It's an important Ending Gambit because it accomplishes two things: First it enables you to sweeten the deal you've made with the buyer, and second, you can use it to get the buyer to agree to things that he or she wouldn't have agreed to earlier.

Car salespeople understand this, don't they? They know that when they get you onto the lot, there's a kind of psychological resistance that has built up to the purchase. They know to first get you to the point where you're thinking, "Yes, I'm going to buy a car. Yes, I'm going to buy it here." Even if it means closing you on any make and model of car, even a stripped down model that carries little profit for them. Then they can get you into the closing room and start adding on all the other little extras that really build the profit into the car.

So, the principle of Nibbling tells you that you can accomplish some things more easily with a Nibble later in the negotiations. Children are brilliant Nibblers. If you have teenage children living at home, you know that they don't have to take courses on Power Sales Negotiating! But *you* have to—just to stand a chance of surviving the process of bringing them up—because they're naturally brilliant negotiators. Not because they learn it in school, but because when they're little, everything they get, they get with negotiating skills. My daughter Julia, when she graduated from high school, wanted to get a great graduation gift from me. She had three things on her hidden agenda:

1. She wanted a five-week trip to Europe.
2. She wanted $1,200 in spending money.
3. She wanted a new set of luggage.

She was smart enough not to ask for everything up front.

Power Negotiating for Salespeople

She was a good enough negotiator to first close me on the trip, then come back a few weeks later and show me in writing (because people are more likely to believe what they see in writing) that the recommended spending money was $1,200, and get me to commit to that. Then right at the last minute she came to me and she said, "Dad, you wouldn't want me going to Europe with that ratty old set of luggage would you? All the kids will be there with new luggage!" And she got that too! Had she asked for everything up front, I would have negotiated out the luggage, and negotiated down the spending money.

What's happening here is that a buyer's mind always works to reinforce decisions that it has just made. Power Sales Negotiators know how this works and use it to add that little extra profit to the job. That little extra profit that can make the difference between profit and loss.

Why is Nibbling such an effective technique? To find out why this works so well, a couple of psychologists did a study at the racetrack in Canada. They studied the attitude of people immediately before they placed the bet, and again immediately after they placed the bet. They found that before they placed the bet the people were very unsure and anxious about what they were about to do. (I want you to relate this to a buyer for a company that you've never sold to before. You may have done a fine job of selling the buyer on your product and service, but the buyer must be unsure and anxious about the decision to start doing business with you.) At the racetrack, they found out that once the people had made the decision to go ahead and place the bet, suddenly they felt very good about what they had just done and often wanted to double the bet before the race started. In essence, their mind did a flip-flop once they had made the decision. Before they decided, they were fighting it; once they'd made the decision, they supported it.

If you're a gambler, you've had that sensation, haven't you? Watch them at the roulette tables in Atlantic City or Las Vegas. The gamblers place their bets. The croupier spins the ball. At the very last moment, people are pushing out additional bets. The mind always works to reinforce decisions that it has made earlier.

I spoke at a Philadelphia convention when the Pennsylvania lottery prize was $50 million and many of the people in the audience were holding tickets. To illustrate how people's minds work to reinforce the decisions that they have made, I tried to buy a lottery ticket from somebody in the audience. Do you think they would sell me one? No, they wouldn't, even for 50 times the purchase price. I'm sure that, before they bought that ticket, they were unsure and anxious about betting money on a 100 million to one shot. However, having made the decision, they refused to change their minds. The mind works to reinforce decisions that it has made earlier.

So, one rule for Power Sales Negotiators is that you don't necessarily ask for everything up front. You wait for a moment of agreement in the negotiations and then go back and Nibble for a little extra.

You might think of the Power Sales Negotiating process as pushing a ball uphill, a large rubber ball that's much bigger than you. You're straining to force it up to the top of the hill. The top of the hill is the moment of first agreement in the negotiations. Once you reach that point, then the ball moves easily down the other side of the hill. This is because people feel good after they have made the initial agreement. They feel a sense of relief that the tension and stress is over. Their minds are working to reinforce the decision that they've just made and they're more receptive to any additional suggestions you may have.

So, always go back at the end for that second effort. Perhaps you sell packaging equipment, and you're trying to convince your customer that she should go with the top-of-the-line model, but she's balking at that kind of expense. You back off, but come back and Nibble for it before you leave. After you've reached agreement on all the other points, you say, "Could we take another look at the top-of-the-line model? I don't recommend it for everyone, but with your kind of volume and growth potential, I really think it's the way for you to go, and all it means is an additional investment of $500 a month." And you have a good chance of hearing them saying to you, "Well, all right, if you think it's that important, let's go ahead."

Perhaps you sell office equipment and part of your program is an additional investment for an extended service contract, but when you present it, they say, "We're not interested in service warranties. We realize how much profit you make on them and we're in a good cash flow position. When it needs servicing we'll pay for it." At that point, you may be thinking that you're not going to risk the sale for the sake of a service warranty, so you back off. Have the courage before you leave to say, "Could we take another look at that extended service warranty? What you may be missing is the preventive maintenance factor. Your employees will call us much sooner if they know that the contract covers the cost of the call, and our technicians can spot trouble before it starts. Your equipment will last longer because you make this invest-ment now. I really think it's the way to go, and all it means is an addi-tional investment of $45 a month." And you have a good chance of hearing, "Well, all right, if you think it's that important, let's go ahead."

So, now that you've learned the fine art of Nibbling, always con-sider these points as you go into negotiations:

1. Are there some elements that you're better off bringing up as a Nibble, after you have reached initial agreement?

2. Do you have a plan to make a second effort on anything to which you couldn't get them to agree the first time around?

3. Are you prepared for the possibility of them Nibbling on you at the last moment?

**The Counter Gambit.** Look out for people Nibbling on you! There's a point in the negotiation when you're very, very vulnerable, and that point is when you *think* the negotiations are all over.

I bet you've been the victim of a Nibble at one time or another. You've been selling a car or a truck to someone. You're finally feeling good because you've found the buyer. The pressure and the tension of the negotiations have drained away. The customer is sitting in your office writing out the check but just as he's about to sign his name he looks up and says, "That does include a full tank of gas, doesn't it?"

You're at your most vulnerable in the negotiations for two reasons:

1. You've just made a sale and you're feeling good. When you feel good, you tend to give things away that you otherwise wouldn't.

2. You're thinking, "Oh, no. I thought we'd resolved every-thing. I don't want to take a chance on going back to the be-ginning, and renegotiating the whole thing. If I do that, I might lose the entire sale. Perhaps I'm just better off just giving in on this little point."

So, you're most vulnerable just after the buyer has made the deci-sion to go ahead. Look out for buyers Nibbling on you. You've made a huge sale and are so excited that you can't wait to call your sales manager and tell him what you've done. The buyer tells you that he needs to call purchasing and get a purchase order number for you. While he's on the phone, he puts his hand over the mouthpiece and says, "By the way, you can give us 60 days on this, can't you? All of your competitors will." Because you've just made a big sale and you're afraid to reopen the negotiations for fear of losing it, you'll have to fight to avoid the tendency to make the concession.

Try to prevent the possibility of a buyer Nibbling on you by:

1. Showing them in writing what any additional concessions will cost them. List extended terms if you ever make them available, but show what it costs them to do that. List the cost of training, installation, extended warranties, and anything else for which they might Nibble.

2. Don't give yourself the authority to make any concessions. Protect yourself with Higher Authority as I taught you in Chapter 4 and the Good Guy/Bad Guy Gambit that I taught you earlier in this book.

When the buyer tries to Nibble you, gently make him feel—cheap! You must be careful about the way you do this because you're at a sensitive point in the negotiation, so smile sweetly and say, "Oh, come on, you negotiated a fantastic price with me. Don't make us wait for our money, too. Fair enough?" Be sure that you do it with a big grin on your face so that they don't take it too seriously!

You also need to know how to prevent post-negotiation Nibbles. Sometimes the buyer wishes she Nibbled on you during the negotiation and so decides to Nibble on you afterward:

1. The buyer agrees to 30-day terms, but deliberately takes 60 days or more to pay.

2. She pays in 30 days but still deducts the Net 15 discount.

3. She requests free additional accounting breakdowns, sometimes just to delay payment.

4. She protests a charge for installation, claiming that you didn't cover this with her.

5. She rejects a charge saying your competition doesn't charge.

6. She contracts for carload shipments, but calls at the last moment to cut the shipment and insist on the carload price.

7. She refuses to pay, or slashes the billing, for engineering charges although during the negotiation she waived this aside as unimportant.

8. She requests extra certifications and is unwilling to pay for them.

You can avoid most of this unpleasantness by:

1. Negotiating all the details up front and getting them in writing. Don't leave anything to, "We can work that out later." Don't be lazy and feel that if you avoid an issue you are closer to making the sale.

2. Use the Gambits to create a climate where the buyers feels that they won. If they feel they won then they are much less likely to Nibble either during the negotiation or afterward.

Power Sales Negotiators always take into account the possibility of being able to Nibble. Timing is very critical—catching the other person when the tension is off and they feel good because they think the negotiations are all over.

On the other hand, look out for the buyer Nibbling on you at the last moment, when you're feeling good. At that point, you're the most vulnerable, and liable to make a concession that half an hour later you'll be thinking—why on earth did I do that? I didn't have to do that. We'd agreed on everything already.

# Key points to remember

➤ With a well-timed Nibble, you can get things at the end of a negotiation that your customer wouldn't agree to earlier.

➤ Nibbling works because the buyer's mind reverses itself after it has made a decision. He or she may have been fighting the thought of buying from you at the start of the negotiation. However, after the decision to buy is made you can Nibble for a bigger order, upgraded product or additional services.

➤ Being willing to make that additional effort is what separates great salespeople from merely good salespeople.

➤ Stop the buyer from Nibbling on you by showing him in writing the cost of any additional features, services, or extended terms; and by not revealing you have authority to make concessions.

➤ When the buyer Nibbles on you, respond by making her feel cheap, in a good-natured way!

➤ Avoid post-negotiation Nibbling by addressing and tying up all the details and by using Gambits that cause them to feel that they won.

# Chapter 19

# Patterns of Concessions

Now let me teach you about **Patterns of Concessions**. If you're involved in extended negotiations over price, be careful that you don't set up a pattern in the way that you make concessions. Let's say that you sell equipment and you've gone into the negotiation with a price of $15,000, but you would go as low as $14,000 to get the order. So, you have a negotiating range of $1,000.

The way in which you give away that $1,000 is critical. There are four errors that you should avoid when making concessions:

**Error Number One: Equal-sized concessions.** This means giving away your $1,000 negotiating range in four increments of $250.

**$250        $250        $250        $250**

Imagine what the buyer's thinking if you do that. He or she doesn't know how far he can push you, all he knows is that every time he pushes he gets another $250. So, he is going to keep on pushing. In fact, it's a mistake to make any two concessions of equal size. If you were the buyer, and a salesperson made a $250 concession, and when pushed made another $250 concession, wouldn't you bet money that the next concession would be $250 also?

**Error Number Two: Making the final concession a big one.** That would be the case if you made a $600 concession followed by a $400 concession.

**$600        $400        $0          $0**

Then you tell the buyer, "That's absolutely our bottom line. I can't give you a penny more." The buyer is thinking that you made a $600 concession, followed by a $400 concession, so he's sure that he can get at least another $100 out of you. He says, "We're getting close. If you can come down another $100, we can talk." You refuse, telling him that you can't even come down another $10 because you've given him your bottom line already. By now the buyer is really upset, because he's thinking, "You just made a $400 concession and now you won't give me another lousy $10! Why are you being so difficult?" So, avoid making the last concession a big one, because it creates hostility.

**Error Number Three: Giving it all away up front.** Another variation of the pattern is to give the entire $1,000-negotiating range away in one concession.

$1,000    $0    $0    $0

You're thinking, "How on earth would buyers be able to get me to give away my entire negotiating range up front?" It's easy! They call you up and say, "You're one of three vendors that we're considering. You're way high right now, but we thought that the fairest way to do this would be to ask all three of you for a 'last and final' bid." Unless you're a skilled negotiator, you'll panic and cut your price to the bone, although they haven't given you any assurance that there won't be another round of bidding later.

Another way that the buyer can get you to give away your entire negotiating range up front is with the "we don't like to negotiate" ploy. With a look of pained sincerity on his face, the buyer says, "Let me tell you about the way we do business here. Back in 1926, when he first started the company, our founder said, 'Let's treat our vendors well. Let's not negotiate prices with them. Have them quote their lowest price and then tell them whether we'll accept it or not.' So, that's the way we've always done it. So, just give me your lowest price and I'll give you a yes or a no. Because we don't like to negotiate here." The buyer is lying to you! He loves to negotiate! That is negotiating—seeing if he can get you to make all of your concessions before the negotiating even starts.

**Error Number Four: Giving a small concession up front to test the waters.** We all are tempted to give a small concession first and see what happens. So, you initially tell the buyers, "Well I might be able to squeeze another $100 off the price, but that's about our limit." If they reject that, you might think, "This isn't going to be as easy as I thought." So, you offer another $200. That still doesn't get you the order so in the next round you give away another $300 and then you have $400 left in your negotiating range, so you give them the whole thing.

$$\textbf{\$100} \qquad \textbf{\$200} \qquad \textbf{\$300} \qquad \textbf{\$400}$$

You see what you've done there? You started with a small concession and you built up to a larger concession. You'll never reach agreement doing that, because every time they ask you for a concession, it just gets better and better for them.

All of these are wrong because they create a pattern of expectations in the buyer's mind. The best way to make concessions is to offer a reasonable concession up front that might just cinch the deal. Maybe a $500 concession wouldn't be out of line. Half of your negotiating range. Then be sure that if you have to make any future concessions, they're smaller and smaller. Your next concession might be $200; and then $100; and then $50.

$$\textbf{\$500} \qquad \textbf{\$200} \qquad \textbf{\$100} \qquad \textbf{\$50}$$

By reducing the size of the concessions you convince the buyer that he has pushed you about as far as you can be pushed.

If you want to test how effective this can be, try it on your children. Wait until the next time they come to you for money for a school outing. They ask you for $100. You say, "No way! Do you realize that when I was your age my weekly allowance was 50 cents? Out of that, I had to buy my own shoes and walk 10 miles to school in the snow, uphill both ways. So, I would take my shoes off and walk barefoot to save money (and other stories that parents the world over tell their children!). No way am I going to give you $100. I'll give you $50 and that's it!"

"I can't do it on $50," your child protests in horror.

Now you have established the negotiating range. They are asking for $100. You're offering $50. The negotiations progress at a frenzied pace and you move up to $60. Then $65, and finally $67.50. By the time you've reached $67.50, you don't have to tell them that they're not going to do any better. By tapering down your concessions, you have subliminally communicated that they're not going to do any better.

**The Counter Gambit.** When you're negotiating, you should always be keeping careful notes. So watch closely for the size of the concessions that the buyer is making to you and write them down. However, don't necessarily feel that the buyer has reached his bottom line because the size of his concessions has narrowed. He may just be using this ploy on you.

## Key points to remember

➢ The way that you make concessions can create a pattern of expectations in the buyer's mind.

➢ Don't make equal-size concessions because the buyer will keep on pushing.

➢ Don't make your last concession a big one, because it creates hostility.

➢ Never concede your entire negotiating range just because the buyer calls for your "last and final" proposal, or claims that he or she "doesn't like to negotiate."

➢ Taper down the concessions to communicate that you are offering the best possible deal.

In Chapter 20 I'll teach you a very effective way of getting a decision from the buyer who is grinding away on you for a better price.

## Chapter 20

# Withdrawing an Offer

As we continue with the Ending Sales Negotiating Gambits let me teach you a very effective technique for concluding the negotiations by **Withdrawing an Offer**. You don't have to use it when the buyer is negotiating in good faith. You use it only when you feel that the buyer is simply grinding away to get the last penny off your price. Or you know that the buyer wants to do business with you, but they're thinking, "How much would I be making per hour if I spent a little more time negotiating with this salesperson?"

Let's say that you sell widgets and you quote the buyer a price of $1.80. The buyer offers you $1.60. You negotiate back and forth and finally it looks as though he or she will agree to $1.72. However, the buyer is thinking, "I got him down from a $1.80 to $1.72. I bet I can squeeze another penny out of him. I bet I can get this salesperson to go at $1.71."

So, he says, "Look, business is really tough right now, I just can't do business with you on widgets unless you can bring the order in at $1.71."

He may be only baiting you, just trying it to see if he can get you down. Don't panic and feel you have to make the concession to stay in the game. The way to stop this grinding away process is to say, "I'm not sure if we can do that or not, but tell you what, if I can possibly get it for you I will." That's a subtle form of the Good Guy/Bad Guy that I taught you in an earlier chapter. "Let me go back; we'll refigure it and see if we can do it. I'll get back to you tomorrow."

The next day you come back, and pretend to withdraw the concession that you made the day before. You say, "I'm really embarrassed about this, but we've been up all night refiguring the price of widgets. Somebody, somewhere down the line, has made a mistake. We had an increase in the cost of raw materials that the estimator didn't figure in. I know we were talking $1.72 yesterday, but we can't even sell it to you for that—$1.73 would be the lowest price that we could possibly offer you on widgets."

What's the buyer's reaction? He's going to get angry and say, "Hey, wait a minute buddy. We were talking $1.72 yesterday and $1.72 is what I want." And immediately the buyer forgets about $1.71. The Withdrawing an Offer Gambit works well to stop the buyer grinding away on you.

You can also employ this Gambit by withdrawing a feature of the offer, rather than going up on price. Here are four examples of that:

1. I know we were talking about waiving the installation charge, but now my people are telling me that, at this price, we just can't.

2. I understand that we were talking about a price including freight, but at a price this low, my estimators are telling me we'd be crazy to do that.

3. I know you requested 60-day terms, but at this price, we'd need payment in 30 days.

4. Yes, I told you that we would waive the charge for training your people, but my people are saying that at this price, we'd have to charge.

Don't do it with something big, because that could really antagonize the buyer. Withdrawing an Offer Gambit is a gamble, but it will force a decision and usually make or break the deal.

**The Counter Gambit.** Haven't we all had an appliance or car salesperson say, "Let me go to my sales manager and I'll see what I can do for you with her." Then he comes back and he says, "Am I embarrassed about this! You know that advertised special we were talking about? I thought that ad was still in effect, but it went off last Saturday. I can't even sell it to you at the price we were talking about." Immediately you forget about future concessions and want to jump on the bandwagon at the price you'd been talking about. Don't let this happen.

When someone uses this on you, don't be afraid to insist that she resolve internal problems first. State that after she has decided who has the authority to make a decision, you will resume the real negotiation.

## Key points to remember

➤ Withdrawing an Offer is a gamble, so only use it on a buyer who is grinding away on you.

➤ You can do it by backing off of your last price concession, or by withdrawing an offer to include freight, installation, training or extended terms.

➤ To avoid direct confrontation, make the Bad Guy a Vague Higher authority. Continue to position yourself on the buyer's side.

## Chapter 21

# Positioning for Easy Acceptance

The **Positioning for Easy Acceptance** Gambit is very important, particularly if you're dealing with buyers who have studied negotiating. If they're proud of their ability to negotiate, you can get ridiculously close to agreement and the entire negotiation will still fall apart on you. When it does, it's probably not the price or terms of the agreement that caused the problem, it's the ego of the buyer as a negotiator.

What you may not realize is that just before you showed up in his office, he said to the person in charge of the purchasing department, "You just watch me negotiate with this salesperson. I know what I'm doing and I'll get us a good price."

Now he's not doing as well as he hoped in the negotiation, and he's reluctant to agree to your proposal because he doesn't want to feel that he lost to you as a negotiator. And that can happen, even when the buyer knows that your proposal is fair and it satisfies his needs in every way.

So, when this happens you must find a way to make the buyer feel good about giving in to you. You must Position for Easy Acceptance. Power Sales Negotiators know that the best way to do this is to make a small concession just at the last moment. The size of the concession can be ridiculously small and you can still make it work because it's not the size of the concession that's critical, but the timing.

You might say, "We just can't budge another dime on the price, but I tell you what. If you'll go along with the price, I'll personally supervise the installation to be sure that it goes smoothly."

Perhaps you were planning to do that anyway, but the point is that you've been courteous enough to position the buyer so that he can respond, "Well all right, if you'll do that for me, we'll go along with the price." Then he doesn't feel that he lost to you in the negotiation—he felt that he traded off.

Positioning for Easy Acceptance is another reason why you should never go in with your best offer up front. Because if you have offered all of your concessions already, before you get to the end of the negotiation, you won't have anything left with which to position the buyer.

Here are other small concessions that you can use to position:

1. A free training class on how to operate the equipment.
2. If you sell office equipment, offer to inventory their supplies and set them up on an automatic reordering system.
3. Hold this price for 90 days in case they want to duplicate this order.
4. Forty-five day terms instead of 30 days.
5. Three years for the price of two on an extended service warranty.

Remember it's the timing of the concession that counts, not the size. It can be ridiculously small and still be effective. Using this Gambit, Power Sales Negotiators can make the buyer feel good.

**The Counter Gambit.** If the buyer makes a token concession to you with the hope that it will appease you, call his bluff. Don't let him get away with it. You might respond with, "I appreciate your willingness to make a concession to me, but a token concession like that is not going to make the problem go away. Remember that I have to sell this to my people. Give me a reasonable concession that I can take to them and have a chance of selling to them. Fair enough?"

## Key points to remember

> ➤ If the buyer is proud of her ability to negotiate, her egotistical need to win may stop you from reaching agreement.
> ➤ Position the buyer to feel good about giving in to you with a small concession made just at the last moment.
> ➤ Because timing is more important than the size of the concession, it can be ridiculously small and still be effective.

# Chapter 22

# Writing the Contract

Now we're at the end of the verbal negotiating and it's time for **Writing the Contract**. In a typical negotiation you verbally negotiate the details and then put it into writing later for both parties to review and approve. I've yet to run across a situation where we covered every detail during the verbal negotiation. There were always points that we overlooked when we were verbally negotiating that we had to detail in writing. Then we had to get the other side to approve or negotiate the points when we sat down to sign the written agreement. That's when the side that writes the contract has a tremendous advantage over the side that doesn't.

Chances are that the person writing the agreement will think of at least half-a-dozen things that did not come up during the verbal negotiations. That person can then write the clarification of that point to his or her advantage, leaving the other side to negotiate a change in the agreement when asked to sign it.

So, don't let the other side write the contract because it puts you at a disadvantage. This applies to brief counter-proposals just as much as it does to agreements that are hundreds of pages long. For example, a real estate agent may be presenting an offer to the sellers of an apartment building. The seller agrees to the general terms of the offer but wants the price to be $5,000 higher. At that point, either the listing agent who represents the seller, or the selling agent who represents the buyer, could pull a counter-proposal form out of his or her briefcase. The agent will write out a brief counteroffer for the seller to sign that the selling agent will present to the buyer for approval. It doesn't have to be complicated: "Offer accepted except that price to be $598,000," will suffice.

However, if the listing agent writes the counteroffer she might think of some things that would benefit the seller. She might write, "Offer accepted except that price to be $598,000. Additional $5,000 to be deposited in escrow upon acceptance. Counteroffer to be accepted upon presentation and within 24 hours."

If the selling agent were to write the counteroffer, he might write, "Offer accepted except that price to be $598,000. Additional $5,000 to be added to the note that the seller is carrying back."

These additions are probably not big enough to be challenged by either a seller or a buyer who is eager to complete the transaction. However, they substantially benefit the side who wrote the brief counteroffer. If the person who writes a one-paragraph counteroffer can affect it so much, think how much that could affect a multipage contract.

Remember, this may not just be a matter of taking advantage of the other side. Both sides may genuinely think that an agreement had been reached on a point whereas the interpretation may be substantially different when it is written out. A classic example of this is the Camp David accord, signed by President Carter, President Anwar Sadat of Egypt, and Prime Minister Menachem Begin of Israel. After many frustrating days of negotiating at Camp David where they all felt until the last moment that their efforts were futile, they reached what they thought was a breakthrough. Excitedly they flew to Washington and with massive publicity signed the accord. In the East Room the normally unemotional Menachem Begin turned to his wife and said, "Mama, we'll go down in the history books tonight." That may be so but the truth is that many years later, hardly any of the elements of the agreement had gone into effect. Their enthusiasm led each of them to think that they had reached agreement when they really hadn't.

If you are to be the one writing the contract, it's a good idea to keep notes throughout the negotiation and put a check mark in the margin against any point that will be part of the final agreement. This does two things:

1. It reminds you to include all the points that you wanted.
2. When you write the contract, you may be reluctant to include a point in the agreement unless you can specifically recall the other side agreeing to it. Your notes will give you the confidence to include it even if you don't remember it clearly.

If you have been team negotiating, be sure to have all the other members of your team review the contract before you present it to the other side. You may have overlooked a point that you should have included, or you may have misinterpreted a point. It's common for lead negotiators to let their enthusiasm overwhelm them to a point where they feel that the other side agreed to something when it was less than clear to more independent observers.

I'm not a big believer in having attorneys conduct a negotiation for you because so few of them are good negotiators. They tend to be confrontational negotiators because they're used to threatening the other side into submission, and they are seldom open to creative solutions because their first obligation is to keep you out of trouble, not make you money. Remember that in law school, lawyers-in-training don't learn how to make deals, only how to break deals. However, in our litigious society there isn't much point in making an agreement that won't hold up in court, so it's a good idea to have the agreement approved by your attorney before you have it signed. One reason for this is that when you prepare the contract, you take on a responsibility. If anything in the contract is unclear, a judge would fault the side that wrote the contract, and you would lose in court on that point. So, in a complicated agreement what you prepare and have the other side sign may be no more than a letter of intent. Have the attorneys work on it later to make it a legal document. It's better that you devote your energy to reaching agreement.

Once the verbal negotiations are over, get a memorandum of agreement signed as quickly as possible. The longer you wait before the other party sees it in writing, the greater the chance that he or she will forget what was agreed to and question what you've prepared.

Also, make sure the other party understands the agreement. Don't be tempted to have a person sign something when you know he or she is not clear on the implications. If something goes wrong, the other party will never accept responsibility and you will be blamed.

I find it helpful to write out the agreement I want before I go into the negotiations. I don't show it to the other side, but I find it helpful to compare it to the agreement that we eventually reach, so that I can see how well I did. Sometimes it's easy to get excited because the other side is making concessions that you didn't expect to get. Then your enthusiasm carries you forward and you agree to what you feel is a fantastic deal. It may be a good deal but unless you have clearly established your criteria, it may not be the deal you hoped for.

If you have prepared an agreement that you think the other side may be reluctant to sign, you may be smart to include the phrase: "Subject to the right of your attorney to reject the contract for any legal reason," to encourage them to sign it. If they're still reluctant to sign, you might broaden that expression to: "Subject to your attorney's approval."

Now the contract has been put in writing and it's time for you to sign it. It's a sad fact, but in this age of computer generated contracts you have to reread a contract every time it comes across your desk. In the old days, when contracts were typewritten, both sides would go through it and write in any changes and then each person would initial the change. You could glance through the contract and quickly review any change that you had made or agreed to. Nowadays with computer generated contracts, we're more likely to go back to the computer, make the change, and print out a new contract.

Here's the danger. You may have refused to sign a clause in a contract. The other side agrees to change it and says they'll send you a corrected contract for your signature. When it comes across your desk, you're busy so you quickly review it to see that they made the change you wanted and then turn to the back page and sign it. Unfortunately, because you didn't take the time to reread the entire contract, you didn't realize that they had also changed something else. Perhaps it was something blatant such as changing "FOB factory" to "FOB job site." Or it may be such a minor change in wording that you don't realize the importance of it until years later when a problem comes up.

Yes, I agree with you—you have a wonderful case for a lawsuit that the other side defrauded you—but why expose yourself to that kind of trouble? Also, realize that if you don't discover it until years later you may not even remember what you agreed to and you can only assume that because you signed it, you must have agreed to it.

In this age of computer generated contracts you should read the contract all the way through, every time it comes across your desk for signature.

**The Counter Gambit.** If the other party jumps first to be the author of the contract, I'll say to that person, "Look, we need to put this down in writing; but let's not go to a lot of expense on this. I have an attorney on retainer, so it won't cost either one of us anything for me to have my attorney do it." Even if I had to pay the attorney to do it, I still think I'd be better off to be the one who is writing the contract.

## Key points to remember

➢ A huge advantage goes to the side that is writing the contract, because when you start to write out the agreement, you will think of several things that you didn't think of when you were verbally negotiating. If you're writing the contract you can write those points to your advantage. When the other side reviews the contract, they will have all their energy tied up in trying to renegotiate those points with you.

➢ Take notes as you're negotiating and put a check mark next to points that you will want to include in the final agreement. It will remind you to include them. Also, you won't be reluctant to include them because you will be certain that you did cover the point during the negotiation.

➢ If you are team negotiating, have your team members review your notes. In your eagerness to reach agreement, you may have assumed that the other agreed to something that they really didn't.

➢ Before you sign a contract, you must read the current version all the way through. The other side may have changed something in that agreement, hoping that you wouldn't catch it.

# Why Money Isn't As Important As You Think

## Chapter 23

# Buyers Want to Pay More, Not Less

After almost two decades of training salespeople, I have become convinced that price concerns salespeople more than it does the people to whom they sell. I'll go even further than that—I think that customers who may be asking you to cut your price are secretly wishing that they could pay more for your product. Please hear me out before you dismiss this as being ridiculous. First, realize that extravagance is a matter of perspective. What you may think is a great deal of money may seem like a bargain to the buyer.

When I was in my early 30s, I was the merchandise manager at the Montgomery Ward store in Bakersfield, California. Although Bakersfield was not a large town, the store ranked 13th in volume in a chain of more than 600 stores. Why did it do so well? In my opinion, it was because head office left us alone and allowed us to sell to the needs of the local population. For example, we did a huge business in home air conditioners because of the outrageously hot summers. In Bakersfield in the summer, it's common for it to be 100 degrees at midnight. In those days an average blue-collar home in that city cost around $30,000. The air conditioners that we would install in these homes might cost $10,000 to $12,000. It was very hard for me to get new salespeople started selling in that department because they had a real resistance to selling something that cost more money than they had ever made in a year. They simply didn't believe that anybody would spend $12,000 to put an air conditioner in a $30,000 home. The customers were willing to pay it, as was illustrated by our huge sales volume, but the salespeople weren't willing to support these decisions because they thought it was outrageously expensive.

However, if I could get a new salesperson to where he began to make big money and he installed an air conditioner in his own home, suddenly he didn't think it was so outrageous any more, and he would dismiss the price objection as if it didn't exist.

Beginning stockbrokers have the same problem. It's very hard for them to ask a client to invest $100,000 when they don't know where lunch money is coming from. Once they become affluent, their sales snowball. I believe that price concerns salespeople more than it does the buyer.

One of my clients is a designer and supplier of point-of-purchase sales aids and displays. (Point-of-purchase means anything that sells the product when the customer is face-to-face with it. It could be packaging, or it could be an automobile showroom television screen that shows the extra features available on the car models.) She told me that if three products are on a shelf in a store—let's say three toasters—and the features of each are described on the carton, customers would most frequently select the highest-price item—*unless* a salesperson comes along to assist them with the selection. When that happens, the salesperson, who is probably working for minimum wage, is unable to justify spending money on the best and manages to talk the customers down to the low-end or middle-of-the-line toaster.

The most important element at point-of-purchase is the description on the carton. The second most important element is the atmosphere in the store. The carton must give customers a reason for spending more money. The atmosphere in the store must convince them that they couldn't buy it for less anywhere else. If you can do those two things, buyers want to spend more money, not less.

I think that spending money is what Americans do best. We love to spend money. We spend $6 trillion a year in this country, and if we could walk into a store and find a salesclerk who knew anything about the merchandise, we'd spend $7 trillion a year. And that's when we're spending our own hard-earned after-tax dollars. What if you're asking a corporate buyer to spend the company's money? There's only one thing better than spending your own money, and that's spending your company's money. If that weren't enough, remember that corporate expenditures are tax deductible, so Uncle Sam is going to pick up 40 percent of the bill.

So, I believe that we've had it all wrong for all these years. When we're trying to sell something to somebody, she doesn't want to spend less money; she wants to spend more. However, you do have to do two things:

1. You must give her a reason for spending more.
2. You must convince her that she cannot get a better deal than the one you're offering her.

That second point, convincing the buyer that they couldn't get a better deal is what Power Sales Negotiating is all about. Everything I teach is designed to convince the other person that he won the negotiation and that he couldn't have done better. Let's face it, does what you pay for something really matter? If you're going to buy a new automobile, does it matter if you spend $20,000 or $21,000? Not really, because you'll soon forget what you paid for it, and the slight increase in payments will not affect your lifestyle. What really matters is the feeling that you got the best possible deal. You don't want to tell your co-workers, "I worked out a terrific deal. I got them down to $21,000," and hear somebody say, "You paid what? My friend bought one of those, and he paid only $20,000. You should have gone to Main Street Auto Mall." That's what hurts—the feeling that you didn't get the best deal.

The objection that every salesperson hears most is the price objection. "We'd love to do business with you, but your price is too high." Let me tell you something about that. It has nothing to do with your price. You could cut your prices 20 percent across the board and you'd still hear that objection.

I trained the salespeople at the largest lawnmower factory in the world. You probably own one of their products because they manufacture most of the low-end private label lawn mowers that discount stores sell. Nobody can undercut their production cost on lawn mowers. They have it down to such a science that if you bought one of their mowers at Home Depot and you tipped the clerk who carries it to your car two dollars, the clerk made more on the lawnmower than the factory did. That's how slim their profit margins are. However, when I asked them to tell me the number-one complaint they hear from the buyers at stores, guess what they told me? You've got it. "Your prices are too high."

You hear that complaint all the time because the people you're selling to study negotiating skills too. They go to their association conventions and sit in the bars saying things like, "Do you want to have fun with salespeople? Just let them go through their entire presentation. Let them take all the time they want. Then when they finally tell you how much it costs, lean back in your chair, put your feet up on the desk, and say, 'I'd love to do business with you, but your prices are too high.' Then try not to laugh as they stammer and stutter and don't know what to say next."

Instead of letting this kind of thing work you up into a sweat, adopt the attitude that negotiating is a game. First, you must learn the rules of the game. Then, you must practice, practice, and practice some more, until you get good at it. Then, you must go out there and play the game with all the gusto you can muster. Negotiating is a game that is fun to play, when you know what you're doing and have the confidence to play it with vigor.

The next time you're trying to get somebody to spend money, remember that they really want to spend more money with you, not less. All you have to do is give them a reason and convince them that there's no way they could get a better deal.

# Chapter 24

# Things That Are More Important Than Money

A reporter once asked astronaut Neil Armstrong to relate his thoughts as Apollo 11 approached the moon. He said, "How do you think you'd feel if you knew you were on top of two million parts built by the lowest bidder in a government contract?" It was a cute line, but he was echoing a popular misconception that the government must do business with anybody who bids the lowest price. Of course that's not true, but it's amazing how many people believe it. I hear it all the time at my Secrets of Power Negotiating seminars: "What can we do when we have to deal with the government? They have to accept the lowest bid."

I once sat next to a Pentagon procurement officer on a flight to the East Coast, and I raised this point with him. "All the time I hear that the government has to buy from the lowest bidder. Is that really true?"

"Heavens no," he told me. "We'd really be in trouble if that were true. Cost is far from the top of the list of what's important to us. We're far more concerned with a company's experience, the experience of the workers and the management team assigned to the product, and their ability to get the job done on time. The rules say that we should buy from the lowest bidder who we feel is capable of meeting our specifications. If we know that a particular supplier is the best one for us, we simply write the specifications to favor that supplier."

So even with the federal government, price is far from the most important thing. When you're dealing with a company that doesn't have legal requirements to put out a request for bids, it's far from the top of the list. Just for the fun of it, review the following list of things that are probably more important than price to buyers:

> ➤ **Being convinced** that they are getting the best deal you're willing to offer.

➤ **The quality of the product or service.** Salespeople frequently tell me that the product they sell has become a commodity. They tell me that their buyers don't care from whom they buy. They only want the lowest price. That's baloney. Would you buy anything in the world based only on the price? Would you go down to the hardware store and buy a nail if the only thing you knew about that nail was that it was the cheapest nail in the world? Of course not.

If it were true that buyers only bought the lowest price product or service, 90 percent of vendors would be out of business. If that were true, the only company that could exist in the market would be the one offering the lowest price, and that's a nonsensical proposition. Realize that it's a smart negotiating strategy for the buyer to convince you that he sees your product as a commodity. It's probably not what he really feels.

➤ **The terms that you offer.** Many large companies make more on the financing of their product than they do the sale of the product. I recently leased a top-of-the-line luxury automobile and became convinced that making the car was only a small part of what this company did. The real money was in financing the lease or the purchase.

➤ **The delivery schedule that you offer.** Can you get it to them when they need it and be counted on to keep doing that? Do you offer a just-in-time delivery system? Are you willing to let them warehouse the product and bill them as they use it?

➤ **The experience you have in delivering the product or service.** Are you familiar with their type of company and the way they do business? Are you comfortable with that kind of relationship?

➤ **The guarantee that you offer and how well you stand behind what you do.** I once paid several hundred dollars to buy a product from a Sharper Image store. After a few months, a part on it broke, and I called their 800 number to see if they would take care of the problem. After listening to me only long enough to understand what the problem was, the operator said, "If you'll give me your address I'll FedEx a replacement part to you." I said, "Don't you need to know when and where I bought it? I'm not sure that I can find my receipt." "I don't need to know any of that," he told me. "I just want to be sure that you're happy with what you bought." When a company stands behind what they do to that extent, am I really going to worry about whether they have the lowest price or not? Of course not.

➤ **Return privileges.** Will you take it back if it doesn't sell? Will you inventory their stock and do that automatically?

➤ **Building a working partnership with you and your company.** The old adversarial relationship between vendor and customers is disappearing as astute companies realize the value of developing a mutually beneficial partnership with their suppliers.

➤ **Credit.** A line of credit with your company may be more important than price, especially to a startup company or in an industry where cash flow is cyclical, and you could take up the slack during the lean months.

➤ **Your staff.** When the contract calls for something to be made (aerospace, construction) or a service to be performed (legal, audit or accounting work, computer services) other factors may be more important than price:

1. The quality of the workers whom you will assign to the job.
2. The level of management that you will assign to oversee the work.

➤ **The ability and willingness to tailor** your product and packaging to their needs.

➤ **The respect that you will give them.** Many times a company will move from a large vendor to a smaller one because they want to be a substantial part of the vendor's business. They feel that it gives them more leverage.

➤ **Peace of mind.** AT&T keeps my telephone business although they are more expensive than Sprint and MCI and have never pretended otherwise. I stay with them because the service has been trouble-free and simple to use for many years, and I have more important things concerning me than switching long distance companies to save a few pennies a call.

---

> ➤ **Reliability.** Can they trust that the quality of your product and service will stay high?

In conclusion, let me remind you that price is not as important as you think it is. Just because you're a salesperson you can conclude that you are exacerbating the price problem. The buyer may make a big issue of price with you because he thinks he'll get a better deal if he does that. But don't be lured into thinking that this is the most important issue on his mind. Far from it.

## Chapter 25

# Finding Out How Much a Buyer Will Pay

In the two previous chapters, I made the point that money isn't the most important thing to consider when you're selling. Now let's look at some techniques to find out the buyer's highest price. When you are selling, the negotiating range of the buyer ranges from the wish price (what they're hoping you'll sell it to them for) all the way up to the walk-away price (the highest price they are willing to pay). How do we uncover the buyer's walk-away price?

Let's look at some techniques that you could use to find out how much a buyer is willing to pay. Let's say that you sell switches to computer manufacturers. Here are some techniques that you could use:

➢ **Raise their top offer by hypothesizing what your higher authority might be willing to do.** Perhaps they buy similar switches now for $1.50 and you're asking $2. You might say, "We both agree we have a better quality product. If I could get my boss down to $1.75, would that work for you?" Protected by Higher Authority, it doesn't mean that you have to sell them to him for $1.75. However, if he acknowledges that $1.75 might be workable, you have raised his negotiating range to $1.75 so that you're only 25 cents apart instead of 50 cents.

➢ **Determine their quality standards by offering a stripped down version.** "We may be able to get down below $1.50 if you don't care about copper contacts. Would that work for you?" In this way, you probably get them to acknowledge that price isn't their only concern. They do care about quality.

➢ **Establish the most they can afford by offering a higher quality version.** "We can add an exciting new feature to the switch, but it would put the cost in the $2.50 range." If the buyer shows some interest in the feature, you know that he could pay more. If he says, "I don't care if it's diamond plated. We can't go over $1.75," you know that fitting the product to a price bracket is a critical issue.

➢ **Remove yourself as a possible vendor.** This disarms the buyer and may cause her to reveal some information that she wouldn't if she thought you were still in the game. You say, "Jane, we love doing business with you, but this item is just not for us. Let's get together on something else later." Having disarmed Jane in this way, a little later you can say, "I'm sorry we couldn't work with you on the switches, but just between you and me what do you realistically think you can buy them for?" She may well say, "I realize that $1.50 is a lowball figure, but I think I'll get somebody to come down to around $1.80."

So the buyer has a wish price and a walk-away price. Going into the negotiation, you won't know what his walk-away price is, because he's going to focus on his wish price. But by using these techniques, you should be able to discover his walk-away price.

As you can see from all we've talked about in this section, there's a lot to be said about the subject of price.

## Key points to remember

➢ Don't exacerbate the price problem by assuming that price is uppermost in the other person's mind.

➢ Don't fall into the trap of thinking that what you sell is a commodity. That's just a negotiating strategy that the buyer is using on you. You do not have to sell for less than your competitor's price to get the sale.

# Section Six

# Secrets of Power Sales Closing

## Chapter 26

# The 4 Stages of Selling

The first thing that a Power Closer understands is that closing tactics do only one thing: They get a decision from the buyer faster than the buyer would otherwise give it. That's a major advantage because the faster you can get someone to decide, the more chance you have of getting what you want. The longer you give a person to think about it, the less chance you have of getting what you want.

Some salespeople have been to one of those ABC sales seminars—you know the "Always be Closing" philosophy—so they start closing from the moment they approach the customer. That's too soon. Others use closing tactics only when they realize that the buyer is not going to say yes. That's too late. Unless you realize that getting a faster decision is the only thing that closing tactics do for you, you won't be a Power Closer because your timing will be off.

Power Closers know that there are four stages to making the sale:

1. **Prospecting**—Finding people who have a need or want for your product or service.

2. **Qualifying**—Finding people who can afford your product or service. Selling is a business, not a religion or a social service. You can't afford to spend time with people who can't afford what you have to offer.

3. **Desire-building**—Making people want your product or service more than anybody else's, and more important, want to do business with you more than anybody else. This is an essential step. If you close before you have built desire, you are simply trying to force the buyer to buy something

that she doesn't yet want. Trying to force her to buy something she doesn't yet want is hard work and means you'll have to drop your price to get the sale. It never leads to satisfied customers—it leads to customers who feel tricked or pressured into buying.

**4. Closing**—Getting the decision from the buyer.

If you're always conscious of the four stages—prospecting, qualifying, desire-building, and closing—you'll be a more powerful closer because the correct timing of the close will empower you.

# Chapter 27

# 24 Power Closes

So, now that you know *when* to close, let me teach you *how* to close using my Power Closes.

## The Tugboat Close

If you've ever stood on a levy at New Orleans, you've no doubt marveled at the tugboats that haul the barges down the Mississippi River. A tiny tugboat no more than 30 feet long can pull a string of barges, each one weighed down with more than 10,000 tons of cargo. When I sail my sailboat near Los Angeles harbor I watch with amazement as a tiny tugboat maneuvers a 300,000-ton super-tanker. What's the secret of the tugboat's incredible power? The tugboat skipper knows that he can move the largest load if he does it a little bit at a time. If he tried to force that super-tanker to change its direction, he couldn't do it. However hard he revved up his engines and attacked that supertanker, he would only bounce off. A little bit at a time, he can do the most incredible things.

What does this have to do with closing a sale? Doing a little bit at a time, you can do the most amazing things. A little bit at a time, you can move the most intractable buyer around and get him to buy from you.

I once got a $250,000 loan from a banker using the Tugboat Close. I owned 33 houses with another investor and I wanted to buy him out so that I would own them all. To do it we needed to get this banker to make a $250,000 loan secured only by a second mortgage on the property. At first, the bank refused to make such a risky investment. The other investor and I asked to meet with the vice president who only restated his position. However, we gently persisted knowing that as long as he wouldn't throw us out, we were getting closer to getting the loan approved. An hour later he had agreed to make the loan if we would cross-secure it with a $100,000 certificate of deposit. We continued to restate our position without any confrontation, knowing that we were nudging him around. Another hour later he agreed to make the loan secured only by the property.

The next time you're in a selling situation where you're convinced that the buyer will never change his mind, think of that tugboat nudging that huge oil tanker around. Buyers do change their minds. Just because he told you no a minute ago, an hour ago, or yesterday, doesn't necessarily mean that he'll say no again if you ask him one more time. A little bit at a time, you can change anyone's mind.

## The Paddock Close

When I was a teenager, I attended the London School of Photography for two years. During my vacations, I earned extra money by photographing thoroughbred horses for breeders. This is a unique branch of photography because the breeders don't want any photographic style. They need a photograph that looks like any other photograph of a horse at stud, so that the breeders can accurately evaluate it. It's a side shot with the far legs of the horse slightly advanced so that the breeders can see all four legs.

It's difficult to get temperamental thoroughbred stallions to stand that way. If you lead the horse in front of the camera and he's not standing properly, you can tug on his leg all you want, but he'll just put it back the way he decided to stand in the first place. That's the way some salespeople try to change their customer's mind—with brute force.

The only way to change the way the stallion was standing was to get his mind off the way he decided to stand before. So I would lead him around the paddock, talking gently to him to get his mind off the decision he had made earlier. Then I would lead him back in front of the camera and see how he was standing now. If he still wasn't standing the way I wanted him to, I would patiently lead him around the paddock once more and try again.

Some buyers are like those stallions. They say no to you for no better reason than that horse decided to stand with its legs together.

When that happens remember the stallion and take them for a mental walk around the paddock. Don't try to force them to change their minds. Instead, tell a little story to take their mind off the decision they made. Think to yourself, "I asked the right closing question but my timing was off. I'll distract them and return to the closing question in a few minutes." After you've mentally walked them around the paddock, go for the close again. If they still say no, walk them around the paddock again, and after you've distracted them with a story, go for the close again.

Great salespeople can do that five or six times without becoming frustrated. Excellent salespeople can do it 10 or 12 times and persist. So never think of a no as a refusal—simply think of it as a sign that you need to walk the buyer around the paddock one more time.

## The "That Wouldn't Stop You" Close

This is the simplest close that I'm going to teach you and it will probably seem ludicrous to you. Until you've tried it, you won't believe how powerful it can be.

My son Dwight taught it to me when he was selling new cars. Whenever he had a customer raise an objection, instead of trying to argue that the customer was wrong or find a way to work around the objection, he learned to say, "But that wouldn't stop you from going ahead today would it?" At first, he felt stupid doing it because he was sure that the customer would ridicule him. However, he discovered that a remarkable number of times the buyers would back away from the objection.

They would say, "You only have the car in red? We wanted green."

He would respond, "But that wouldn't stop you from going ahead today would it?"

And they would say, "Well no, I guess it wouldn't."

It sounds outrageous, doesn't it? But if you try it, I think you will end up kicking yourself because you'll find that objections that have been giving you fits for years really don't need a response.

The buyer says, "Your competitor will sell me widgets for 10 cents less than this."

You say, "But that wouldn't stop you from buying from us would it?"

He may well say, "Well I guess not, if your service is as good as you promised."

The mark of a Power Closer is that she knows that she doesn't have to satisfy every objection. If you decide to do that you'll begin to feel that you're in a shooting gallery where every time you knock down one objection, another one pops up.

## The You Can Afford It Close

My travel agent used this close to get me to spend $7,000. With the right person in the right circumstances, I think it's very powerful.

A few years ago, my daughter Julia and I decided to spend a month in Africa. The trip would include a climb of Mount Kilimanjaro in Tanzania and a visit to a game preserve in Kenya. Just before we left, we happened to see the movie *Gorillas in the Mist*, the story of Diane Fosse's fight to save the almost extinct mountain gorillas in Rwanda. Fascinated by this I called my travel agent Tess Vizon to see if we could visit the gorillas while we were in Africa. She started checking and called me back a few days later. "There are only 29 silver back gorillas left in the world," she told me. "They are all in the area in Central Africa where Rwanda, Uganda, and Zaire meet. Because they are so few and none of them are in captivity, it's almost impossible to visit them. However, the brother of the President of Zaire owns a small lodge up in mountains and I can get you in the week before Christmas. It will cost you an extra $7,000 dollars to do it."

When I heard the price, I almost choked. We were not naturalists with a lifetime ambition to see these gorillas. All we'd done was go see a movie and become curious about them. "Tess," I said, "I'm not sure I want to pay $7,000 to see some gorillas."

Her response was brilliant. She said, "Oh come on, Roger. You want to do it. You can afford to do it. Go ahead and do it."

I thought that it was one of the best closes I'd ever heard. Of course she flattered me by thinking that I had that much money to throw around, but the truth was that I could afford to do it and I did want to do it. So I told her to book it and it turned out to be the highlight of our trip.

Remember the You Can Afford It Close when you're dealing with affluent customers. It's very effective, and they will appreciate being flattered. And probably, they'll enjoy what you sold them and never miss the money.

## The Leave 'Em Alone Close

When I was a teenager in England, I sold appliances for a living and frequently sold to husbands and wives. I learned that I could really raise my closing percentages if I left them alone for a few minutes toward the end of my presentation. If I stayed with them the whole time, I risked losing the sale. You see, however well they knew each other, they couldn't read the other person's mind. They weren't sure if their spouse wanted to buy or not. Leaving them alone for a while gave them a chance to ask, "What do you think dear?"

This doesn't apply only to husbands and wives. You might be selling to the president and vice president of a company. The president may be eager to go ahead but he or she wants to be sure that the vice president is "on board" and will enthusiastically support the investment. Or the vice president may be eager, but isn't sure if the president will overrule her. Give them some time alone to resolve those issues and closing the sales will be easier for you.

Once I learned the art of leaving them alone for a while, much of my problem in closing sales went away. The larger the item the more important this becomes. Real estate, for example, is such a major decision that this close may be indispensable.

Don't make your buyers ask you for time to talk it over, give it to them. Just be sure that they're in the closing room or in your car, not near their car where they can easily leave. You don't have to say, "Let me give you time to think about it." Simply find an excuse to leave them for a few minutes, such as fetching coffee or looking for a piece of paper.

## The Vince Lombardi Close

This is a terrific close for add-on items such as extra features or extended warranties. It also works well for moving buyers up to the top of the line. When you're selling, a psychological resistance sometimes builds up in the buyers' mind. As buyers approach the point of making a decision, they start to resist spending the money. Perhaps they feel guilty; perhaps they feel anxious that they may be doing the wrong thing, or that they're not getting the best deal. Whatever the reason the tension builds until the moment they make the decision. Then, once they have made the decision to purchase, a remarkable change takes place in their mind. Having made the decision to buy, their mind does anything it can to reinforce the decision that they just made. That's when you can get them to add-on extras or move up to the more expensive model.

Car salespeople know this, don't they? They know that if they can close you on any make and model of car, even a stripped down one, then they can get you into the closing room and add-on all the other little extras that really build the profit into the car.

So, one rule of Power Closing is that you do not have to close on everything up front. Once you reach that point of agreement, the buyer stops being your opponent and becomes your partner in the sales process. That's when you can make the second effort and add-on all of those profitable extras.

Vince Lombardi always used to talk about the second effort, didn't he? He loved to show his Green Bay Packers film clips of receivers who almost caught the ball but couldn't quite hang onto it. But instead of letting it go, they made a second effort and caught it before it hit the ground. Or running backs who were tackled but still managed to wriggle free and make the touchdown. Vince Lombardi would tell his players that everybody is out there making the first effort. They wouldn't be on the team if they didn't know how to play the game well and were out there doing everything that he told them to do. But everybody's doing that. Every team in the league is doing that. The difference, Vince Lombardi would say, between the good players and the great players is that the great players will make that second effort. When everyone else thinks that the play is lost, they'll still keep trying.

You wouldn't be selling for your company if you didn't know how to sell and if you weren't out there doing everything that your manager expects of you. But that's only going to make you a good salesperson. If you want to be a great salesperson, take a tip from Vince Lombardi: When everyone else is saying, "Give up. You've tried hard enough," give it one more effort.

# The Silent Close

The Silent Close is always a fun one to use. The principle is to make your presentation and then shut up! From then on, the first person who talks loses.

Buyers can respond to your sales proposal in one of three ways: They can say yes, they can say no, or they can let you know that they can't decide. If you're a positive thinker, you expect them to say yes. You will be surprised if they say no, or that they can't decide. So, wait to find out. Until you find out that they won't say yes, don't change your proposal.

I once made an offer on an apartment building to a seller who was asking $240,000. My offer was $180,000. Frankly, it scared me to death to present an offer that low. I thought the seller would be furious that I wasted his time. I gritted my teeth and read the offer to him. Then I turned the offer around, pushed it across the desk, and laid my pen on top of it for him to sign.

He looked at it for a while, and then he picked it up and read it all the way through, including the fine print. He put it down and looked at me. I bit my tongue to stop myself from talking.

He picked the offer up again and read it all the way through. Then he put it down and looked at me again, for what seemed like five minutes.

Finally he said, "I suppose that now I'm supposed to say yes, no, or maybe. Is that right?"

I smiled slightly but still didn't say anything. He picked it up for the third time and read it all the way through. Then he said, "I'll tell you what I'll do. I won't accept this but I will accept this." He wrote a very acceptable counter-proposal on the bottom of the offer, turned it around, and slid it back across the desk to me.

The Silent Close is the simplest to understand and one of the hardest to use. We're not used to silence. Even a minute of silence seems like an eternity.

Remember: always assume the customer will say yes. Don't say a word until you find out whether they will or whether they won't.

## The Subject To Close

The Subject To Close is a great way to handle buyers who are intimidated by the size of the decision that you're asking them to make. In real estate, we understood that when our customers were buying a new home, it was probably the largest investment they would ever make. We knew that we had found the perfect home for them, but sometimes the enormity of the decision would stop them from going ahead. I would teach our agents to say, "Why don't we just write it up subject to you being approved for the financing?" By making the sale conditional on another event taking place, you appear to be turning a major decision into a minor one. Naturally, a good real estate agent knows that you will qualify for the financing, so you really have bought.

The life insurance agent realizes that his buyer is having trouble agreeing to his proposal. He says, "Frankly, I don't know if I can get this much insurance on someone of your age. It would be subject to your passing the physical, so why don't we just write up the paperwork subject to your passing the physical." It doesn't sound as though you've made as big a decision as you really have. However, the agent knows that if his customer can fog a mirror during that physical, he can find someone, somewhere, who will underwrite that policy. The customer really has bought.

## The Contingency Close

You use the Subject To close when you know that buyers can pass the contingency. They will qualify for the financing, or they will be able to pass the underwriter's physical. But what if you don't know that the buyer will pass the contingency successfully?

What if the only way the real estate agent can get the buyer to make an offer is subject to the sale of the buyer's present home? What if the equipment salesperson is forced to write up the offer subject to his credit department carrying the paper at prime rate? Can it still be effective even if the contingency is one that he can never overcome?

Yes, it's probably still the smart thing to do, even if the contingency seems insurmountable, because you're psychologically drawing buyers closer to making the decision. When their mind is drooling at the thought of ownership, it's easier to get them to remove the contingency. Just be sure that you're not using it as a closing crutch. Only write up a contingency offer as a last resort.

# The Ben Franklin Close

I'm sure that you've heard of the Ben Franklin Close before. It's based on something Franklin wrote to British chemist Joseph Priestley about the way that he made decisions. He wrote:

> *"My way [of making decisions] is to divide a sheet of paper into two columns, writing over the one Pro, and over the other Con. Then, during the three or four days' consideration, I put down under the different heads short hints of the different motives that at different times occur to me, for or against the measure. When I have thus got them all together in one view, I endeavor to estimate their respective weights, and where I find two, on each side that seem equal, I strike them both out. If I find a reason pro equal to some two reasons con, I strike out all three. If I judge some two reasons con, equal to some three reasons pro, I strike out the five, and thus proceeding I find at length where the balance lies, and if, after a day or two of further considerations, nothing new that is of importance occurs on either side, I come to a determination accordingly."*

The Ben Franklin Close is designed to make people feel better when they have trouble making up their mind. When using this as a closing technique there is an essential preamble. Unless you use the preamble, the Ben Franklin Close won't work. So, before you use the close you say, "Mr. Buyer, I'm not surprised that you're having trouble making a decision because many intelligent people do. For example, one of our greatest statesmen, Ben Franklin, had trouble making decisions. Let me tell you what he used to do. See if you think it's a good way for you to make up your mind. When Ben couldn't make up his mind he would simply take a sheet of paper and draw a line down the middle. On the left-hand side he'd list all the reasons for going ahead with the project and on the right-hand side, he would list all the reasons for not going ahead with the project. If the reasons for going ahead exceeded the reasons for not going ahead, he would decide to proceed. Doesn't that make sense for you too, Mr. Buyer?" It's important to get the buyer's agreement that he will go along with this method before you go ahead with the analysis. If you don't, you can go through the entire exercise and still have him tell you that he wants to think it over.

Having gotten his agreement that it's a good way to decide, start listing the reasons for his going ahead with the investment. On this side of the list, give him all the help you can. "Didn't you like this? Didn't you like that?" Help him make that lefthand column as long as it can be. However, when you exhaust the reasons for going ahead and start on the reasons for not going ahead, he's on his own. Doing it like this, your list of positives has to exceed the list of negatives and you'll get the buyer's agreement.

## The Dumb Mistake Close

Sometimes you'd like to climb over the desk and tell the buyer what a dumb mistake they're making when they're reluctant to buy. You can't do this, of course, because it would antagonize the buyer. The Dumb Mistake Close is a way of telling buyers what a dumb mistake they are making without actually accusing them of it. The difference is that you tell them a story about someone else who made a dumb mistake when they were in the same situation.

Perhaps you sell real estate and your buyers are balking at the high payments. You might say, "You know what I wish? I wish Roger Dawson were here. He tells the story on one of his tapes about the first house he ever bought. He went down to the bank to sign the loan papers and realized that he would be committing to pay $67 a month for 30 years. He started to figure out what a huge commitment that was and got cold feet. Fortunately, the loan officer realized the problem, took pity on him, and broke the rules by saying, "You have to go ahead. The papers are all prepared." So like an obedient little boy he went ahead and signed the papers. Within a few years, the house doubled in value. If Roger were here now, he'd tell you to close your eyes and sign. It seems like a great deal of money now, but five years from now, it won't. You'll look at it as the smartest move you ever made."

I remember buying a bicycle for my son John when he was young. This was before helmets became mandatory for cyclists in California. After we'd picked out the bike the store owner selected an expensive

24 *Power Closes*

helmet and said, "You'll need this, too." Of course, my son's safety concerned me but I had ridden a bike throughout my childhood and none of my three children had ever had a helmet before, so it seemed like an unnecessary expense. The storeowner said, "Oh I wish Mr. Jones was here now. He lives up on Skyline Drive and last month he bought a bike for his son Bobby. He didn't want to invest in a helmet either. The next day he was riding down Church Hill Drive and went straight into a car coming up the hill. He was seriously injured and for the rest of my life, I'll have to live with the knowledge that I didn't insist on him getting a helmet. I wish Mr. Jones were here now, because he'd tell you how important it is." Guess who grabbed that helmet out of her hands and rammed it onto his son's head? You've got it! The Dumb Mistake Close is a terrific way to pressure the buyer without confrontation.

## The Final Objection Close

To make the Final Objection Close work you have to appear defeated, as though you've given up trying to sell them. "Okay," you say, "I accept that you're not going to buy from me, but just to clarify my thinking, would you mind telling me why you decided not to go ahead? What did I do wrong?"

"You didn't do anything wrong," the buyer will tell you. "You did a good job."

"Then it must be my company or the quality of my product."

"No, that's not it either. It's just that your price is higher than our current supplier."

"Well that makes me feel better," you say. "Price isn't something I can do anything about. I'm glad it wasn't anything I did. So the only reason you're not going ahead is the price?"

Once you've narrowed it down to the Final Objection by removing the appearance of still trying to close, you have only to answer that objection to make the sale. For this close to work you must go through these four stages:

1. Appear defeated.
2. Release the pressure.
3. Get them to narrow it down to one objection.
4. Overcome that objection.

143

## The Puppy Dog Close

I'm sure that you've heard the story of the pet store owner who's trying to sell the little boy a puppy. When the boy says he can't decide, the owner suggests that he take the puppy home for the weekend, telling him, "If you don't like him you can bring him back on Monday." He's sure that by Monday the little boy will have fallen in love with the puppy and won't dream of bringing him back.

Back in the 1950s, my first sales job was in an appliance store where we sold thousands of televisions using the Puppy Dog Close. In those days, television was new to most people and you might be the only person on your block to have one. Your neighbors even expected you to invite them over to watch it and serve them tea and sandwiches. If we had a potential customer who couldn't decide, we would suggest that he take it home for a trial. We knew the minute the neighbors saw the antenna being erected on the roof, they would be asking if they could come over to watch television. How could they not keep the television after the neighbors had been over to spend the evening watching it?

At the real estate company that I ran, I would encourage the sales associates to carry an instant camera with them. When a buyer made an offer on a new home, we would take a picture of them in front of the house knowing that they would show the picture to their friends and relatives. Then if the owner wouldn't accept the buyer's offer, we knew that the buyer was much more likely to raise their offer. Who wants to tell their friends that they couldn't afford to pay more?

## The Minor Point Close

When you're selling, little decisions lead up to big decisions. If you can get your customer to agree on minor points, you are clarifying their thinking so that when you get ready for the major decision, they are less likely to feel pressured.

The car salesperson asks the buyer:

➤ "If you did go ahead would you want leather or vinyl upholstery?"
➤ "Would you want the stick-shift or the automatic?"
➤ "Would you prefer white or red?"

The real estate salesperson asks:

> ➢ "If you chose this home, which of these bedrooms would be the nursery for your new baby?"
> ➢ "How would you arrange the furniture in the living room?"

## The Positive Assumption Close

This may seem obvious to you, but it's essential to assume that the buyer is going to buy from you. It amazes me how many salespeople, particularly novices, make a negative assumption—they seem surprised if the buyer says yes! If you walked into a restaurant and the server came up and asked you if you *wanted* to order food, she would confuse you wouldn't she? She knows what you're there for and simply assumes that you're going to buy food. You should do the same thing with your customers. Always assume that they're going to buy.

I believe that fear of the customer not buying is at the heart of high-pressure selling, and it's why customers hate high pressure. There's no need to high-pressure customers when you assume that they will buy. High-pressure tactics come only from salespeople who fear that customers are not going to buy unless they force them to.

So, keep your conversation positive. Say, "You like the looks of this model, don't you?" not "Do you like the way it looks?"

Say, "I'm going to include the extended service warranty because the small investment is really going to pay off for you," instead of "Do you want the extended warranty?"

Always make positive assumptions—that they're going to buy, that they're going to buy from you, that they're going to buy today, and that everything is going to go through without a hitch.

## The Return Serve Close

This close teaches you that when the buyer asks you a question, you should usually reply with a question. Many years ago, I was buying a used copy machine from an attorney. I asked, "Would you take $200 for it?" He said, "Are you offering me $200?" I thought, "How smart." If he'd have told me instead that he would take $200, I probably would have hemmed and hawed around before offering him even less. When buyers look as though they're close to making a decision to buy and serve you a clarifying question, return the serve and in doing so, you'll be getting a commitment. When the buyer says, "Does it come in black?" say, "Would you like it in black?" "Can you give me 45 days to pay?" should cause you to respond, "Would you like 45 days to pay?"

## The Prisoner of War Close

This close is very effective with people who can't make up their mind. It requires you to relate a true and interesting fact to your buyers. I'm sure you're aware that during World War II there were many stories of prisoners of war escaping from German prisoner of war camps. However, during the Korean War there were very few attempts to escape. The reason was that the Chinese psychologically evaluated their prisoners for their decision-making abilities. They found that only 10 percent of them were comfortable making decisions and these they kept in solitary confinement. They kept the other 90 percent in compounds where they were virtually unguarded and yet none of them attempted to escape. Explain to your buyers that the ability to make good decisions under pressure is rare so they shouldn't feel bad that they are having trouble making a decision.

At that point, they will decide that they are part of the 10 percent who do have the courage to make a decision and decide to go ahead. Or they may acknowledge that they are part of the 90 percent that does have trouble, in which case you explain that that's what you're there for. You're the expert and they should let you make the decision for them.

## The Alternate Choice Close

When you ask people to choose between one of two alternatives, they will usually pick one of the two. Very seldom will they select the third option: that neither of the two choices is acceptable.

Frankly, whenever I use the Alternate Choice Close, its effectiveness surprises me all over again. Before customers have made a decision to buy I will say, "If you did go ahead, would you use your American Express Card or your MasterCard?" They nearly always pick one of the two. Then I say, "Would you like me to fill out the form for you, or would you rather do it yourself?" With just a couple of quick alternate choice questions, I have closed the sale. The interesting thing is that even if they know what you're doing, people seem irresistibly drawn to picking one of the two alternatives. (Be sure that both of the options are acceptable to you. "Do you want it or not?" is not a smart alternate choice!)

This is such a well-known close that you'll even hear little children using it. "Dad, would you like to take me to the video arcade tonight or would tomorrow night be better for you?" As a grandson goes into the ice cream store he says, "Grandpa, are we going to get doubles or triples today?"

Also use the Alternate Choice Close for setting appointments. Assume that the buyer wants to see you and ask, "Would Monday or Tuesday be better for you?" "Would 10 o'clock or 11 be better for you?"

Be sure that you have narrowed the choices down to two. It won't work with three options so you need to eliminate the third option. If you sell cars you might say, "I think the first one we looked at would be too small for you so it's between the red one and the white one. Which did you prefer?" If you sell real estate and you've shown the buyer three properties, you might say, "I got the feeling that you didn't like the master bedroom in the first house, so if you were going to go ahead with one of the other two, which one would it be?"

You can use the Alternate Choice Close to handle objections also. Perhaps you sell real estate and the buyer says, "We would never buy this house. Look at those awful green walls." So, you respond with the Alternate Choice question, "So if you did go ahead, would you repaint the walls yourself, or would you have a painter do it?" Whichever choice he makes, you've won, haven't you? He can brag that he can do the job much better and cheaper than a painter can, or he can tell you that he has better things to do with his time. It doesn't matter what he says because either way you have eliminated the objection.

## The Doorknob Close

Like the Final Objection Close, the Doorknob Close is dependent upon being able to release the buyer from the pressure of the buying decision.

When you have tried everything else and still don't have the order, close your briefcase and say, "It was really nice talking with you even though you decided not to go ahead. I can understand your feeling about that. Perhaps sometime in the future we can get together again." You appear to be leaving but as your hand hits the doorknob on the way out of their office, you pause pensively and say, "Would you mind helping me? I always try to learn something whenever I fail to make a sale. Would you mind telling me what I did wrong? It will help me so much in the future."

As long as they feel that you're no longer trying to sell them, they'll often be helpful enough to share with you why they didn't buy. They may say, "You came on too strong, too early. We felt pressured." Or they may say, "We liked what you were showing us but we just can't afford it and we didn't want to tell you that the payments would be a struggle for us."

Now you can move to the Vince Lombardi Second Effort Close. Gently thank them for sharing and slide back into your presentation. Remember that the Doorknob Close will only work if you're able to convince them that you're no longer trying to sell them. You're only asking for their help on how to improve your presentation.

# The Divide and Conquer Close

You may have to use the Divide and Conquer Close any time that you are trying to sell to two people. I've noticed that frequently opposites attract when it comes to assertiveness levels. A less assertive person will often marry a more assertive person. A businessperson who has a warm and easy-going personality—a people person—will often have a much more assertive business partner. They make a good team. The assertive no-nonsense person admires the warm human qualities of the less assertive person. The easy-going people person admires the discipline and firmness of the more assertive person. You'll notice that assertive people are fast decision-makers. They will look at a proposal and go for it, or not go for it, quickly. Less assertive people agonize over decisions and that analysis frequently leads to paralysis.

When you're faced with this, you should use the Divide and Conquer Close. Get the more assertive person aside and say, "Mrs. Jones, I really admire the analysis that your husband, Roy, is doing here. I wish I had that kind of detailed mind. But what concerns me, Mrs. Jones, is that you're going to lose this opportunity if you don't decide to go ahead now, and you do want to do it, don't you?" Then she'll go to her husband who is still imputing the whole thing into his computer and say, "Roy, knock it off for heaven's sake. It's a great opportunity and we need to jump on it."

Similarly with business partners, you may have to find a way to get the more assertive one aside and say, "I get the feeling that you're the decision-maker around here, Bob. Let's move on it before it's too late." Chances are, he'll say something like, "Don't worry about it. You have a deal. I just have to be diplomatic about the way I handle it with Kathy."

So whenever you're selling to two people and one of them is more assertive than the other, use the Divide and Conquer Close. Find a way to separate them and get the decision from the more assertive partner.

## The Let 'Em Think Close

With some people, it's easy to tell when they're thinking. They use a pad of paper and fill it with numbers and options, or they pull out a calculator and punch in numbers furiously. With others, it's harder to tell when they're thinking because they quietly work out the decision in their mind. That's a problem for salespeople because salespeople can't stand silence. They think it means that the customer has lost interest and needs you to stimulate the deal with conversation. Sometimes you have to give people time to think.

I remember when I was investing heavily in income-producing real estate. Many times an agent would take me out to show me an apartment building that he or she wanted to sell me. In the car on the way back, I would need time to think it through. How much would it cost me to improve the property? How high could I raise the rents? Where would I generate the cash for the down payment? How would I handle the management? I prefer to do all this in my mind and verify my calculations later. To the agent it must look as though I'm totally disinterested. All too often, the agent would interpret this as meaning that he or she had to give me more information to stimulate my interest. Nothing could be further from the truth. I simply needed some quiet time to think about it.

Soon we would be back at the agent's office and I couldn't give them a decision because I didn't have time to think. So, don't kill your sales by talking too much. As Samson would tell you: The jawbone of an ass is for killing Philistines, not for killing sales.

## The Bank Note Close

If you sell investments, you'll get a kick out of the drama of the Bank Note Close. You use it when your investor turns down an investment opportunity because he or she thinks that something better will come along.

Take a $20 bill out of your pocket, drop it on the floor, and put the toe of your shoe on it. Then say, "Let me ask you this. If you were walking along the sidewalk and saw a $20 bill lying there, would you pick it up? Of course, you would. It's an opportunity that exists for you, just as the investment I showed you is an opportunity. You wouldn't pass up the opportunity to pick up the $20 bill because there may be a $50 bill lying further down the sidewalk, would you? But that's exactly what you're doing if you pass up an opportunity as good as the one I showed you today!"

The Bank Note Close is a whimsical one, and you can fault the logic, but the drama of the bank note on the floor will often give your investor the impetus that it takes to make him or her say yes.

## The Recall Close

I learned this close as a teenager when I was selling televisions in England. Although we didn't have much sales training in those days, I quickly figured out that it wasn't good to tell customers everything you knew about the product. It was smart to leave something out that you could suddenly recall in case you're not able to close them.

Perhaps I would demonstrate a television to them and they would show interest in it but tell me that they wanted to look in some other stores before they made up their mind. I would wish them the best of luck and then, just as they approached the door on the way out of the showroom, I would call out, "Just a minute folks. I just recalled that I didn't show you something very important about this television. Did you know that the wood finish on the cabinet is completely resistant to cigarette burns? You can grind out a cigarette on it and it won't damage it. Let me show you." Then I would lead them back to the television, demonstrate the feature, get back into my sales presentation, and go for the close again.

Whatever you sell, don't tell the customer all the benefits of ownership. Always leave something out for the Recall Close. Perhaps you sell cars and you don't tell them about the special lock that enables the driver to unlock her door without unlocking the passenger door. Then you can call them up and say, "I can't believe this but I just recalled that I didn't tell you something very important. I'd like to come by this evening and show it to you. Would 7 or 8 o'clock be better for you?" You've heard of buyer's remorse of course, but non-buyer's remorse is a reality, too. They may be sitting there thinking, "I wish we'd brought that car home with us today." They still want to be sold because they feel guilty spending that much money, so they may not be willing to call you. However, they welcome it when you call them and give them a second chance to invest.

## The Take Control Close

Some people have a terrible time making a decision. There are people out there who find making a decision so traumatic that they won't make a move until someone tells them to. In transactional analysis terms, these people are the "child" personalities. Psychologist Eric Berne took Freud's theory of super ego, id, and ego and simplified it into parent, child and adult. The superego (or parent) restrains the other two parts of the personality. The id (or child part of the personality) tends to act impulsively without thought. The ego (or adult part of the personality) reasons things through.

You would think that the impulsive childlike personality would be the easiest to sell to. After all, their philosophy is: If it feels good do it. However, over the years this has gotten them into trouble. So now they may really want your product and service but they can't decide because they're afraid of the trouble they may get into. In other words, they have cold feet.

These people need to be told to buy.

You tell them firmly, "I'm not going to leave here today until I get your permission to go ahead. Everything tells me that this is the right decision for you. I can't leave here today in good conscience without getting your okay, so I'm going to make the decision for you. Just sign here and I'll take care of the details."

Of course, you can only do this if you're convinced that they should. Don't do it just to earn a commission. However, if you're totally convinced that they'd be making a mistake to say no, this extra push of decisiveness may be the only way you can get them to do the right thing.

# The Dawson Pledge

You might call the Dawson Pledge the last resort. If everything else has failed, I want you to take the Dawson Pledge. You note the time on your watch and you mentally raise your left hand, put your right hand over your heart and think, "I hereby pledge that I will not leave these buyers until one more hour has gone by." Whatever it takes, and even if you never mention your product or service for one more hour.

Ask for another cup of coffee—that'll take five minutes. Pretend it's too hot to drink and you can get 10 minutes out of it. Maybe the pot is empty. That's good. Make them brew another one. Now you're talking a half-hour. Whatever it takes, don't leave for one more hour.

As Power Sales Negotiators know, the longer you can keep someone engaged, the more flexible they become. Just because they're telling you no now, doesn't mean that they won't be saying maybe 30 minutes from now, and yes an hour from now.

So, if all else fails, take the Dawson Pledge.

# Chapter 28

# Questionable Closes

Now let me cover a couple of questionable closing tactics, so that you can defend yourself when they're used on you.

## The Deliberate Mistake Close

As with any con job, the Deliberate Mistake requires a victim who also lacks ethics. The buyer baits the hook when he or she prepares a proposal and deliberately leaves out one of the requirements or leaves the quality standards vague on one of the elements.

Perhaps the element left out is the cost of stamping serial numbers, something the salesperson knows the law requires for recall purposes. The vague quality standard might be the requirement for copper-tipped switches. In either case, a knowledgeable salesperson would spot the mistake. An ethical salesperson would immediately point out the omission to the buyer.

If the salesperson is unethical, however, he may go ahead and offer a low price that gets him the sale. He feels secure knowing that he can come back later and raise the price to cover the additional items that the buyer will eventually need.

However, the sting is on, as they say in the movies. Eager to close the sale before the buyer discovers the omission, the salesperson becomes a sloppy negotiator and may well make concessions that he wouldn't normally, because he knows that he can make it up later when the omission is uncovered. However as soon as they make the deal and the buyer and salesperson are shaking hands, the buyer pulls the sting and says, "By the way, you realize that we're required to have serial numbers stamped on them, and copper-tipped switches, don't you? That's standard in the industry and I'm sure you'll get that done for us." Hoisted by his own petard, the poor salesperson is too embarrassed to admit his deceit and goes along with the concessions.

In reverse, the Deliberate Mistake is the car salesperson who runs an adding machine tape on the cost of the car but only includes the price of a tape player, when the car also has a CD player. If the customer takes the bait, he or she starts thinking that they now have an opportunity to put one over on the car salesperson. They become eager to close the deal before the salesperson spots the mistake. This eagerness makes the customer a sloppy negotiator and he or she may end up paying more for the car than if he or she had pointed out the mistake. Apart from that, the salesperson still has the option of "discovering" the mistake before the buyer consummates the sale and with an accusing look, shames the buyer into paying the extra amount.

The Counter Gambit may sound high-minded but it's obvious. Never try to get away with anything. If your greed doesn't cost you at that moment, it will certainly catch up with you later down life's road. Instead, point out the mistake and say, "I assume that you're not charging me for the CD player because you're trying to get me to make a decision now?"

# The Erroneous Conclusion Close

A variation of the Deliberate Mistake is the Erroneous Conclusion Close. Using this method, the salesperson asks the buyer a question but deliberately draws an erroneous conclusion. When the buyer corrects the salesperson, he or she has made a commitment to buy. For example, the car salesperson says, "If you did decide today, you wouldn't need to take delivery today, would you?" The buyer responds, "Well, of course we'd want to take it today."

The real estate salesperson says, "You wouldn't want the sellers to include the refrigerator would you?" The buyers hadn't been thinking of doing that but the refrigerator looks better than theirs does so they reply, "Do you think they would include it?" The salesperson responds with, "Let's include it in our offer and see what happens."

The boat salesperson says, "You wouldn't expect us to include a cover, would you?" The buyer sees an opportunity to get something for nothing and responds, "I sure would."

# Section Seven

# How to Control the Negotiation

# Chapter 29

# Negotiating Drives

You probably don't think much about what is driving the buyer because you tend to assume that what drives the buyer is the same thing that drives you, which is getting the best deal. Sociologists call this "socio-centrism," meaning that you tend to feel that the buyer wants what you would want, if you were them. Power Sales Negotiators know that what we would want, if we were them, may have nothing to do with what the buyer really wants.

Poor negotiators get into trouble because they fear that they will be vulnerable to the buyer's tricks if they let the buyer know too much about them. Instead of wanting to find out what is driving the buyer and revealing his or her drives to the buyer, the poor negotiator lets his fears stop him from being that open.

Power Sales Negotiators know that the better we can understand what drives the buyer—what the buyer really wants to accomplish—the better we can fulfill the buyer's needs without taking away from our position.

Let's look at the different things that drive the buyer when he or she is negotiating with you. Recognizing and understanding these drives is a major key to win-win negotiating.

## The Competitive Drive

This is the drive that salespeople know best and it's why they see negotiating as being so challenging. If you assume that the buyer is out to beat you by any means within the rules of the game, of course you will fear meeting a buyer who might be a better negotiator than you or someone who is more ruthless than you.

The Competitive Drive certainly exists at most car dealerships. The car dealer attracts customers by offering "the lowest prices in town" but pays its salespeople based on the amount of profit they can build into the sale. It's a gladiatorial approach to negotiating: The customer wants to buy for the lowest price even if the dealer loses money and the salesperson loses his commission, and the salesperson wants to drive the price up because that's the only way he can make any money. Sound the trumpets, let the spectacle begin, and may the best person win.

Competitive Drive negotiators believe that you should find out all you can about the buyer but let the buyer know nothing about you. Knowledge is power but Competitive Drive negotiators believe that because of this, the more you find out and the less you reveal, the better off you'll be.

When gathering information, the Competitive Drive negotiator distrusts anything the buyer might tell him because it may be a trick. He gathers information covertly by approaching the other employees at the buyer's company. Because he assumes that the buyer is doing the same to him, he works assiduously to prevent the leaking of information from his side.

What's causing this approach is the assumption that there has to be a winner and there has to be a loser. What's missing is the possibility that both sides could win because they are not out for exactly the same thing; and by knowing more about the buyer, you can concede issues that are important to the buyer but may not be significant to you.

## The Solutional Drive

This is the best negotiating situation and the one we all enjoy. This is when the buyer is eager to find a solution and is willing to calmly discuss with you the best way to do that. It means that both sides will negotiate in good faith to find a win-win solution.

Solutional Drive negotiators tend to be wide open to creative solutions because they feel that there must be a better solution out there somewhere that hasn't occurred to them yet. It takes an open mind to be creative. Just look at some of the variables that buyers and sellers could propose in a simple transaction such as buying a house:

1. The cost of financing to the buyer could be adjusted by letting the buyer assume an underlying loan. Or the seller could carry back all the financing and remain liable for the underlying loan (called wrapping the underlying).
2. The buyers could accommodate the sellers by giving them more time to move out or find another home. The sellers could even lease back the house from the buyers for an extended term.
3. The price could include all or some of the furnishings.
4. The sellers could retain a life estate in the house that would enable them to stay in the house until they die. This is a great idea for elderly people who need cash but don't want to move.
5. The broker's fee could be renegotiated, or the broker could be asked to take his fee in the form of a note, rather than in cash.
6. The buyer could move in but delay the closing to help the seller with income taxes.

The great thing about negotiating with someone who is in the Solutional Drive is that they have cast nothing in stone. Company policy or tradition does not restrict them—they feel that everything is negotiable because everything was at one time negotiated.

Short of breaking the law or their personal principles, they will listen to any suggestion you care to propose because they do not see you as being in competition with them.

It sounds like the perfect solution doesn't it? Both sides cooperating to find the perfect and fair solution. However, there is one caveat. Buyers might be feigning when they appear to be in the solutional drive. Once you have put your cards on the table and told them exactly what you are prepared to do, they may revert to Competitive Drive negotiating. So, if it seems too good to be true, be wary.

## The Personal Drive

You may encounter situations where the buyer's main drive is not to win for winning's sake, or to find the perfect solution. The main drive may be for his personal profit or aggrandizement.

A case that quickly comes to mind is that of an attorney who is working on a fee basis rather than a contingency basis. The attorney would make more money if it takes a long time to find a solution. True, it might be a better solution, but the improvement may not be worth as much as the extra fees, so you're the one who has to balance your Solutional Drive with the attorney's Personal Drive. When you run into this, you should see what you can do to satisfy the attorney's personal need for more fees. It may be the promise of more business in the future if he can wrap it up quickly.

Or you may have to revert to a Competitive Drive if the attorney is being difficult. If you feel that he's reluctant to support what you feel is a reasonable compromise, it may be in your best interest to threaten to take your solution over the attorney's head to his client. He won't appreciate that, of course, but if he feels that his client would accept the compromise if you went over his head, you may force him to accept your solution.

Another example of the Personal Drive would be a union negotiator who wants to look good to his members. In that case, it may be in both your best interests to make an outrageous initial demand. Then he can go back to his members and say, "So, I wasn't able to get you everything you wanted, but just listen to their opening negotiating position. I was able to get them all the way down from that for you." If you had made a more modest opening negotiating position it might have been difficult for him to sell it to his members because they didn't feel that their union fought hard enough for them.

Another example of Personal Drive would be a young buyer who wants to look good to her company. She may have scheduled an inspection tour of your assembly plant that has cost her company a great deal of time and money. So, the last thing she wants to do is go back empty handed without a signed contract, so if your Drive is Competitive, your best strategy might be to establish that she has a time deadline and stall the negotiations until the last moment.

You might be able to reach a terrific settlement in the limousine on the way to the airport if she'd rather agree to anything than go home empty handed.

# The Organizational Drive

You may find yourself in a situation where the buyer seems to have a fine Solutional Drive. He really wants to find the best solution, but the problem is that it has to be a solution that he can sell to his organization. Because of this, his drive has to be Organizational: Even if he found the perfect solution, could he sell it to his people?

This happens a great deal in Congress where the senator or congressperson is eager for a sensible compromise but knows that he or she would get ravaged by the voters back home. In close votes, you'll see this all the time. On both sides of the house, the politicians who have the support of their voters will commit quickly. Those who will be in trouble in their state or district may want to support their party but are reluctant to toe the line. So, the party leadership counts noses to see how many votes they need to win by one vote. Then they let their members who would be most hurt by voting for the bill, vote no. The ones who would be least hurt are led, like lambs to slaughter it always seems to me, and made to vote for the bill.

When you're negotiating with buyers who must please their organization, they may be reluctant to lay out their problems for you because it would seem too much like collusion. So, you need to be thinking, "Who could be giving these buyers heartburn over this one?" Is it their stockholders, their legal department, or perhaps government regulations that they would have to circumvent to implement the best solution? If you understand their problems, you may be able to do things to make the solution more palatable to their organization. For example, you might take a more radical position with the other people at his company than you do at the negotiating table. In this way, your compromise gives the appearance of making major concessions.

A company hired me once to help out when the assembly workers' union went on strike. The union negotiators felt that the solution they had negotiated was reasonable, but they couldn't sell it to their members who were out for blood. We arranged for the local newspaper to interview the president of the company. During the interview, he expressed sincere regrets that he was caught in a difficult situation. The union couldn't sell the plan to its members and the president couldn't sell anything better to his board of directors and stockholders. It appeared that the strike would soon force him to move production from that factory to their assembly plant in Mexico. The next day the workers' spouses opened up the newspaper to read headlines that said, "Plant to close—jobs going south." By the afternoon of that day, the spouses had put enough pressure on the workers that they clamored to accept the deal that they had previously turned down.

If you're dealing with a buyer who has to sell the plan to his organization you should always be looking for ways to make it easier for him to do that.

# The Attitudinal Drive

The Attitudinal Drive negotiator believes that if both sides like each other enough, they can resolve their differences. The Attitudinal Drive negotiator would never try to resolve a problem by telephone or through an intermediary. This person wants to be face-to-face with the other person so that he or she can get a feel for who that person is, believing that, "If we know each other well enough, we can find a solution."

Former President Jimmy Carter is very much an Attitudinal negotiator. He initiated contact with the North Koreans when they were refusing to back down on their nuclear weapons program. He met with Haitian General Cedras right up to the brink of war and pleaded with President Clinton for just a few more minutes to reason with the General. When he finally reached a settlement he actually invited that bloodthirsty dictator to come to his church in Plains, Georgia, to teach a Sunday school class!

The problem with that kind of negotiating is that it can easily lead to appeasement of the buyer. The Attitudinal Drive negotiator is so eager to find good in the buyer that he can readily be deceived. The classic example of Attitudinal negotiating was when Prime Minister Neville Chamberlain of England made a last ditch effort to avoid war with Adolf Hitler. He returned to England triumphantly proclaiming that he had averted war by giving away only part of Czechoslovakia. Adolf Hitler had already figured out that he was a chump and it didn't take the rest of the world long to agree with Hitler's assessment.

Certainly it helps that the buyer and you like each other because it's hard to find a win-win solution without that. The problem is that this is a two-way street. At the same time that you're working to have buyers like you, the buyers are working to have you like them. If you both like each other so much, you're just as likely to make concessions to them as they are to you. Power Sales Negotiators know that something is far more important than having the buyer like you: You must create a solution that is in both sides' best interests. Then it is mutually beneficial for both of you to support the buying arrangement and see that it flourishes.

In the next chapter, I'm going to teach you the questionable gambits that buyers can use to get you to sweeten the deal. Unless you're so familiar with them that you spot them right away, you'll find that you'll be making unnecessary concessions to the buyer because you think that it's the only way to get the order.

# Chapter 30

# Questionable Gambits and How to Counter Them

Many a salesperson has had to endure an embarrassing interview with a sales manager who can't understand why the salesperson made a concession that the manager didn't think was necessary to get the sale. The salesperson tries to maintain that the only way to get the order was to make the concession. The truth was that the buyer outmaneuvered the salesperson with one of the questionable gambits outlined in this chapter.

There's no point in getting upset with the buyer who does this. You must deal with the world the way it is, not the way you would like it to be. Power Sales Negotiators remember to concentrate on the issues and think of negotiating as a game. The buyer is simply doing his or her job, which is to get the best possible deal from you. The fact that he or she stepped over an ethical boundary shouldn't stop you from doing your job, which is to get the best possible deal for your company. To do that, you need to be skilled enough to recognize these questionable gambits instantly and counter them smoothly.

## The Decoy Gambit

Buyers use the Decoy Gambit to take your attention away from the real issue in the negotiation.

Perhaps you're selling custom gears to a large manufacturer of bulldozers located in Houston. You've been calling on this company for two years trying to get your foot in the door, but they have never been willing to budge from their existing supplier; but today appears to be the day when your persistence will pay off. The buyer offers to give you a large order providing that you can complete shipment in a

90-day period. Both of you know that it typically takes 120 days to design, engineer, and manufacture a custom gear. The thought of getting the sale excites you, but you realize that a 90-day ship date is virtually impossible.

You check with the people at your plant and they confirm that even 120 days would be a scramble and that nonrecurring engineering costs will be $22,000. However much you fight for an accelerated production schedule, you can't get your people to budge. It's going to take 120 days and not a day less—even if that causes you to lose the order.

You return to present the proposal to the buyer. You show him a price of $230,000 for the gears, plus $22,000 in nonrecurring engineering costs, FOB your plant in Toledo, with shipment in 120 days.

The buyer insists that he must have delivery in 90 days to complete a large shipment the company needs to deliver to a construction project in Buenos Aires. The negotiation has taken on an air of two people desperately trying to solve a problem together, but no suggestion seems to solve the problem. The negotiation appears to have stalled.

Finally, the buyer says, "Maybe there's something that would work. Let me check with my shipping people and see what they have to say. I'll be right back." He leaves the office for 15 minutes. Your mind is in turmoil, thinking of the commission that you'll be losing if you can't put this sale together. By the time the buyer returns you're almost frantic.

The buyer has a concerned look on his face and says, "I think I've found a way, but I need your help to put it together. My guy in shipping says that we can air freight the gears to Argentina but we're going to have to pay off some customs people down there. To do this I need you to waive the engineering charges and air freight them to us in Houston at your expense."

Unless you're very careful you'll be so relieved at finding a solution to the problem that you'll concede the $22,000 engineering charge, and agree to pick up a $6,000 air freight bill. And it may be months before you realize that the buyer used the Decoy Gambit on you. Six months later you're sitting in the hotel coffee shop in Dallas talking to a friend of yours who sells sheet metal to the bulldozer company. He asks you how you got your foot in the door and you tell him the story. Your friend says, "I don't believe what the buyer told you. It doesn't ring true to me. Those people have the best-organized manufacturing plant in the business. They always work at least six months out. No way would they be ordering custom gears only 90 days out." Only then does it dawn on you that the shipment date was never the real issue. They could have lived with 120 days. The ship date was the Decoy issue. The buyer created the issue of an accelerated shipment date simply so that he could trade it off later for the real issue: waiving the engineering charges and the freight.

**The Counter Gambit.** Stay focused and isolate the objection: "Is that the only thing that's bothering you?" Then go to Higher Authority and Good Guy/Bad Guy: "Let's get something in writing and I'll take it to my people and I'll see what I can do for you with them." Then turn the tables, "We may be able to accelerate the shipment but it's going to increase the nonrecurring engineering charges."

# The Red Herring Gambit

This is a further twist on the Decoy Gambit. With the Decoy, the buyer raises a phony issue to get concessions on a real issue. With the Red Herring, the buyer gets all upset about a peripheral issue with the hope that it will soften you up to make concessions on a real issue. If the Red Herring distracts you, it will deceive you into thinking that it's of major concern to the buyer, when it may not be.

Red herring is an English foxhunting expression. Animal-rights activists whose prime target was foxhunting found that if they dragged a dried and salted herring (which is a red color) across the path of the hunt, its smell would mask the trail of the fox and confuse the dogs. When it happens, the hunt master will cry, "Those blighters have faulted my hounds with their red herring." In this way the phrase became part of the English language and came to mean the raising of an issue that would divert and confuse opponents. When President Harry Truman faced increasing charges from Congress that communists had infiltrated his administration he responded by saying, "It's just a red herring to get the minds of the voters off the sins of the 80th Congress."

When buyers are creating a red herring issue that they will later be willing to concede, you should keep your eye on the real negotiating issues and don't let them link it to a concession you're not eager to make. For example, you may run into a buyer who is making a big issue about a very minor blemish on the last shipment you sent him. It's so minuscule that it's well within tolerance levels and he has never made an issue of it before. However this time he sounds serious and it looks as though he's going to ask you to accept return of the entire shipment. Then he tells you that he doesn't think he'd have these problems if he was dealing with your competitor and that they're willing to cut their price to get a foot in the door. Now he has you so intimidated that you fear that you'll not only have to refund the shipment but also lose the account. Then when he suggests that he might be willing to overlook all this in return for a price concession, you're in danger of trading off a real issue for one that he had created.

Another example of the Red Herring may be an account that is extremely delinquent in paying her bills. Your vice president of finance sent you down there to get the check or put her on a C.O.D. basis. When you get there, she starts ranting and raving about how your last shipment arrived late and caused her to cancel an entire evening assembly line shift. This astounds you because she never mentioned it before. It's probably just a red herring to distract you from the real issue of collecting payment.

## The Cherry Picking Gambit

A buyer can use this gambit against you with devastating effect, unless you're a Power Sales Negotiator and know your options. Let's imagine that you sell printing and you're bidding on a job for a small appliance manufacturer that includes shipping cartons, display cartons, instruction booklets, feature hang-tags, feature stickers, and store display materials. You bid a lump sum and then follow up to see if you can get the order.

The buyer tells you that he'd like to do business with you, but he has three bids and you're high on your price but he can't figure out why. He asks you to submit a bid broken down by item so that he can evaluate your proposal better. If he's done this with all three vendors, he now has three prices for each item in the proposal. So, he could parcel out the job and have the lowest bidder on each item supply him with that item. Is there anything unethical about that? That's not what you want to happen but there really isn't anything unethical about it. What is unethical is Cherry Picking the bids, which means taking the lowest price on each item and telling the other two bidders that they will have to meet it to be considered. Buyers clearly love Cherry Picking whereas salespeople hate it. Buyers should push for itemized contracts whereas salespeople should avoid it.

Because Cherry Picking is a questionable gambit, the perpetrator is less likely to do it to someone he or she knows and trusts than to a comparative stranger. So, you can forestall this tactic by building a personal relationship with the buyer.

As with any tactic, always consider the alternatives of the other side before making a concession. The fewer alternatives the other side has, the more power you have. If you as a salesperson refuse to budge on your price, you force the buyer to pay more from another supplier, or use multiple suppliers. In the case of the printing job, this would mean that the buyer would in effect become his own jobber and have to contract with each sub-vendor separately. This may require more knowledge or expertise than the buyer possesses or may create so much extra work and pressure that it is not worth the savings. Remember also that when the buyer places all the items in the hands of one supplier, he has much more leverage than if he spreads the work around to several suppliers.

Let's recap the disadvantages of dealing with several suppliers so that you'll hold the line on price the next time a buyer tries to Cherry Pick your proposal:

1. Dealing with several suppliers is a big hassle.
2. If the buyer needs all the items before he can ship the product, he is entrusting the continuity of his assembly process to several suppliers rather than just one.
3. By placing the entire order with one supplier, he can develop influence and power over that supplier.
4. This is the key issue: He doesn't get you to supervise the entire printing process for him.

It's easy for a Cherry Picking buyer to intimidate a neophyte salesperson and until you put yourself in the buyer's shoes, you may not realize how much power you have. What if the buyer said to you, "Your price is far too high on the instruction booklet. Match your competitor's price on that and you can have the job." You reply, "There's no way we can be the low bidder on every item. Take the instruction book out of the bid and give it to the competition." The buyer would probably respond, "I don't want to do that. It's too much of a hassle dealing with multiple vendors. I want one vendor to supply all of the items." Now do you see how much power you have?

## The Default Gambit

The Default Gambit involves a unilateral assumption that works to the advantage of the side proposing it. It's the company that sends a payment check to you after having deducted 2.5 percent. Attached is a note that says, "All of our other vendors discount for payment within 15 days, so we assume you will, too."

It's the salesperson who writes a potential buyer, "Because I haven't heard from you on your choice of options, I will ship the deluxe model unless I hear from you within 10 days."

The Default Gambit preys on busy or lazy people and assumes that rather than take action, these people will take the easy way out and let the perpetrator get away with it. Once a person fails to respond, the law of precedent comes into play and when this person finally does object, the response is, "But you've never had a problem with it in the past."

As with all questionable gambits, call the buyer or seller on it, and gently explain the benefits of establishing a relationship of trust between you.

## The Escalation Gambit

Another questionable gambit is Escalation, which means to raise the price, or change the terms or conditions, after you have struck a deal. I once knew a man who had become very wealthy after he sold his real estate franchise to a large corporation. He had been one of the original purchasers of a territory when real estate franchising was new and the founder of the company was running around the country trying to sign up anyone who believed in his concept. Many years later a huge New York corporation had bought the master franchise and was starting to buy back the territorial franchises. After attending one of my Secrets of Power Negotiating seminars, he asked me to join him for a drink and asked me, "Roger, have you ever heard voices speak to you when you're negotiating?" Not wanting to admit it if I had, I asked him what he was talking about. He told me that after he had agreed to sell his territorial franchise to the new corporate owners for a huge amount of money, he started to have second thoughts. Because his was the first franchise the corporation was buying back, they planned to fly him to New York for a signing ceremony followed by a press conference at which they would announce the corporation's plans to buy back all the franchises. "The night before the ceremony I had trouble sleeping," he told me. "I lay on my bed wondering whether I was doing the right thing. Suddenly I heard a voice talking to me."

"What was it saying?" I asked him, expecting a humorous punch line.

"It said, 'Joey, you're not getting enough money.' So, the next morning I went down and asked for another half-million dollars, and got it."

What Joey was describing was a classic case of escalation—raising demands after both sides have reached agreement. Of course it's outrageous and unethical, but just as Joey thought he heard voices telling him to do it rather than accept responsibility for his actions, the perpetrators often don't see any harm in cutting the best deal by any means possible. So, why is anyone ever allowed to get away with such outrageous behavior? All too often, the other side swallows their pride and concedes just as easily as that corporation conceded the extra half-million. In their case, they paid up rather than face the humiliation of having to call off the press conference. In other cases, the other side has simply become too emotionally involved in the purchase to back out.

The history of big business is full of stories of people who extorted a little more out of a deal simply because they had enough leverage to do so, and frankly I have mixed emotions about how to respond. My heart tells me that if people do that, you should call their bluff and walk away from the deal on principle. However, I also believe in keeping emotions out of a negotiation. If that New York corporation was able to pay the extra half-million and still have it be a good deal (and it was still a *very* good deal) then they were right to swallow their pride and pay the money—provided that the deal didn't include having to continue to do business with the perpetrator. That would be too high a price to pay.

Fortunately, the history of big business is also full of stories of people who would not sell their honor at any price. One morning a man shook hands on a deal to sell his cattle ranch in Orlando. Later that day, the Orlando Sentinel broke the news that Walt Disney was secretly buying up all the land to create Walt Disney World. The rancher could have held out and made millions more, but his sense of honor stopped him from doing it.

When Henry Hollis sold the Palmer House hotel in Chicago to Conrad Hilton, he shook hands on Hilton's first offer of $19,385,000. Within a week, he received offers of more than a million dollars above that, but he never wavered on his word. As Hilton said in his autobiography, "I have done business with a great many men in my time. I do not think I have ever had a greater experience than dealing with this perfect gentleman. I felt throughout that I was watching a master in the greatest traditions of American business."

**The Counter Gambits.** To counter the Escalation Gambit, you might try to:

1. Protect yourself with Higher Authority as I taught you in Chapter 11. Tell them that their suggestion does not offend you, but that your board of directors will never renegotiate a deal once you have made it, and you will be forced to walk away. Then Position for Easy Acceptance, as I taught you in Chapter 21, by telling them that although you cannot budge on the price, you might be able to offer them something of value in another area.

2. Escalate your demands in return. Tell them that you're glad that they want to reopen the negotiations because your side has been having second thoughts also. Of course, you would never renege on a deal, but because they have chosen to negate the original proposal, your price has now gone up also.

It is better to avoid Escalation than to have to deal with it. Avoid it by:

1. Tying up all the details up front. Don't leave anything to "we can work that out later." Unresolved issues invite Escalation.

2. Building a personal relationship with the other side that makes it harder for them to be ruthless.

3. Getting large deposits so that it's harder for them to back out.

4. Building win-win negotiations so that they don't want to back out.

# The Planted Information Gambit

The next questionable gambit you might encounter is Planted Information, which preys on the fact that we tend to believe information that we obtained surreptitiously. I remember flying back from a speaking engagement and discussing that day's presidential press conference with my seatmate. "I don't believe he's telling us the truth," he told me. "I met a man who knew someone who works at the White House and he told me that the president did know all about it all along. He's covering something up." What amazed me about this was that I found myself believing what this man was telling me, rather than believing what I had earlier heard the President of the United States say at the press conference. Why? Because we always tend to believe information that we have obtained surreptitiously.

Planted information can be an astoundingly powerful influencer. Imagine a salesperson is making an impressive presentation to a board of directors. Flip charts and audio visual aids surround him. He is fervently making a plea that they go with his company because he offers the best value in the marketplace. He believes that no competitor can undercut his prices and feels confident that he can close the sale at his asking price of $820,000. Then he sees one of the directors pass a note to another director who nods and lays the note on the table in front of him. Curiosity gets the better of the salesperson. He has to see what's on that note. He finishes his presentation, then approaches the table, and dramatically leans toward them. "Gentlemen, do you have any questions?" Out of the corner of his eye, he can now see the note. Even reading upside down, he can see that it says, "Universal's price is $762,000. Let's go with them."

The chairman of the board says, "I do have one question. Your price seems high. We're obligated to go with the lowest price that meets our specifications. Is $820,000 the best you can do?" Within minutes, the panicked salesperson has lowered his price by $58,000.

Was the note real or was it planted information? Although it was just an unsubstantiated note scrawled on a piece of paper, the salesperson believed it because he obtained the information surreptitiously. If they had planted it, could the salesperson cry foul later? No, because they didn't tell him that the competition's bid was $762,000. He obtained the information surreptitiously and he must accept responsibility for his assumptions.

Simply knowing about planted information will help you to diffuse this questionable tactic. Any time that you're negotiating based on information that is only what the other side has chosen to tell you, you're extremely vulnerable to manipulation. When the other side may have planted the information for you to discover, you should be even more vigilant.

Now I've told you about some of the questionable gambits that you encounter. Remember that the only reason I did this was for your own protection. As always, the best business tactic is to be totally honest and above board. It's not only the right thing to do, it's the smart thing to do.

# Chapter 31

# Negotiating with Non-Americans

At my Secrets of Power Negotiating seminars, I usually get some questions about negotiating with non-Americans. It seems that just about everyone has had a frustrating experience dealing either with a foreigner in a foreign country or a person of foreign origin who lives in this country.

I'm an immigrant from England, and although I've been here more than 30 years and a citizen for more than 20 years, I can relate to the difficulty of dealing with non-Americans. Along with my experience of moving here and adapting to the American way of doing things, I have traveled to more than 100 other countries.

It is easy for non-Americans to misunderstand us. Because of my background, I know how different America is from any other country on earth, and how America is deceptively different to non-Americans. They think they know us from watching our movies and television shows. However, movies and television don't always reveal what is in the American heart and mind and that is what determines our approach to business.

Conversely, we tend to look at non-Americans and think we understand them. True, they may dress in Western business suits and speak our language, but that doesn't mean that their traditional values and mindsets have changed. They may prefer American music and American movies, but their beliefs in their way of life and the values that they place on their traditions are as strong as ever.

I believe that underneath all of our apparent similarities, there are enormous differences in our approach to business. So, let's take some time and attempt to unravel the mysteries of negotiating with non-Americans.

New York real estate investor Donald Trump wrote a best-selling book called *The Art of the Deal* that detailed many of his remarkable real estate negotiations. The title and the premise of the book illuminate what is the overriding concern of most American negotiators—the cutting of the deal. We do live in a very deal-conscious environment.

I suppose that sociologists would tell you that this is because we are such a mobile and diverse society that we have little sense of roots. Instead of trusting the people and the way things are done, as is common around the world, we place all of our trust in creating an unbreakable deal. "Will it hold up in court?" we demand, as though anyone who doesn't consider the possibility of having to defend the deal in court is naive.

Most non-Americans completely reject our dependence on the deal. Should they choose to sign a contract at all, it is simply an expression of an understanding that existed between the parties on a particular date. It is a formal expression of a relationship that now exists between the parties. As with any other relationship, it must mold itself to changing conditions.

It astounds most Americans to learn that you can sign a contract in Korea and have it mean nothing six months later. "But we signed a contract," the American howls. "Yes," their Korean counterpart patiently explains, "we signed a contract based on the conditions that existed six months ago when we signed it. Those conditions no longer exist, so the contract we signed is meaningless."

"Foul," cries the American. "You are trying to cheat me." Not at all. What seems to be disreputable action to us is not to them and we interpret it that way. It is merely their way of doing things.

It often delights Americans who are selling to people from the Middle East that they had so little trouble getting a contract signed. Then they are horrified to find out that in the Arab world, signing the contract announces the start of the negotiations, and not the end. A signed contract means less in their culture than a letter of intent does in ours. It won't surprise you to learn that Americans resort to legal action more quickly and frequently than any other people on earth. This would be laughable to a salesperson in many countries such as India where the civil legal system is close to nonexistent. I am not putting this down, and you shouldn't either. What you should do is recognize that different nationalities and cultures have different ways of doing things, and if you plan to sell to them, it behooves you to learn, understand, and appreciate those ways.

Before you put too much dependence on that contract you signed with a foreign buyer, perhaps you should figure out how you could force him to adhere to it.

Even if you're selling in a country that does have an operative legal system for civil lawsuits, the damage it could do might mean that it's not worth pursuing. In America, legal action is so common that companies continue to do business with a company that is suing them. We see it as a normal way to resolve a dispute and no reason for rancor. In most foreign countries, there is such a loss of face involved in being sued that they will refuse to deal with you in any way once you have sued them.

The context describes the degree of importance attached to the relationship between the parties, as opposed to the details of the contract. When the relationship is paramount, we call it a high context negotiation. When the deal is the thing, we call it a low context negotiation. Different nationalities place greater or lesser importance on context—the environment in which the proposal is made. Cultures listed from high context to low context are: The Orient, The Middle East, Russia, Spain, Italy, France, England, United States, Scandinavia, Germany, Switzerland. From this list, you can see that only Scandinavia, Germany, and Switzerland concentrate more on the content of the deal than Americans do. All other countries care more about the relationship between the parties.

So, the first thing you should learn about negotiating with non-Americans is that the deal is not the major issue to them. They put far more trust in the relationship between the parties. Is there good blood between the parties? Because if there is only bad blood, no amount of legal maneuvering will make the relationship worthwhile. While you're trying to hammer out the fine points of the deal, they are spending time assessing the fine points of your character.

Apart from concentrating more on the deal than on the relationship between the parties, the other major mistake that Americans make in dealing with non-Americans is that we want to get down to business too quickly. Nobody gets down to business faster than Americans do. Typically, we exchange a few pleasantries to ease any tension and then get right down to hammering out the details of the deal. We socialize afterwards. Non-Americans may take days, weeks, or even months before they feel comfortable moving from the getting-to-know-you stage to the point where they feel good about doing business with you.

When the Shah of Iran fell from power, the real estate company that I ran in Southern California did a huge amount of business with Persians who were fleeing the new regime in Iran, often with millions in cash to invest. Often I would watch our people make the mistake of trying to talk business too soon, which caused the Iranians to distrust them. Quickly we learned that they needed time to size us up and wanted to sit and drink tea for several hours before talking business.

If you fly to Japan to conduct business, you may have to socialize for many days before they feel that it's appropriate to talk business. Be careful, however, that they're not just trying to push you up against a time deadline. At my seminars many people have told me that their joy at being treated so well soon turned to chagrin as they realized how difficult it would be to get down to business at all. They have told me horror stories of not being able to negotiate until they were in the limousine on the way back to the airport. True, it's a two-hour ride out to Narita Airport, but that is negotiating under excessive time pressure. Terrified at the thought of going home empty handed, they went straight to their bottom line.

So, you are likely to fall into two major traps when selling to non-Americans: 1) You will overemphasize the deal and not attach enough importance to the relationship of the parties, and 2) You'll get down to business too quickly. The two are closely related of course. Building a relationship with a foreign buyer to the point where you feel comfortable with him takes time. Enlarging on that relationship to the point where you trust him and he trusts you, so that you don't have to rely on the contract being airtight, takes a great deal of time.

Let's look at nine characteristics of the typical American who sells to non-Americans. Of course, this may not describe you accurately, but if you identify with any of these characteristics, you should adapt your approach when selling to non-Americans.

**To a non-American you are probably very direct in your communications.** You use expressions such as "What's your bottom line?" or "How much profit would you make at that figure?" Or you try to shift the emphasis of the negotiations by saying, "Let's lay our cards on the table," or "Let's wrap this one up tonight." Although this kind of directness puts pressure on the other side, realize that to non-Americans it may seem too blunt, and such bluntness will probably offend them.

**Because you're an American, you probably resist making outrageous initial demands.** This goes back to your hope that you can "cut the deal" and "get out of Dodge." Because you want to blitz the negotiations and wrap them up quickly, you tend to think in much shorter time frames than do non-Americans. You're thinking you can conclude the negotiations in hours, while they're thinking it will take many days. A foreigner may make outrageous initial demands because he knows that the price and terms will change enormously as the days go by, but you see that as slowing the negotiations down by drawing you both into endless haggling.

**You are more likely to negotiate alone than a non-American.** It is common to find a lone American negotiator showing up at an international negotiation, fully empowered to do business. (You may be able to put together a team of three if it includes your interpreter and driver.) Then when you get to the negotiating room you find a team of 10 or 12 negotiators from the other side. Of course, this is not good for you, because you'll feel psychologically overwhelmed unless the negotiating teams are roughly the same size. However, the effect of this on the foreign team concerns me more. They see a lone negotiator and may interpret this as "They're not serious about making a deal at this meeting because if they've only sent one negotiator, this must be only a preliminary expedition." Or they get the impression that you're merely gathering information to take back to your team of negotiators. Unless you understand this and take pains to explain that you are the entire negotiating team and that you are empowered (up to a point) to negotiate the deal, they may not take you seriously.

**You are probably uncomfortable with emotional displays.** The English are the worst of course, but Americans also see displaying emotions in public as a weakness. If your wife starts to cry, for example, you probably assume that you have done something devastatingly cruel to her. In the Mediterranean countries, the husband would simply wonder what ploy his wife had concocted. If you fear an emotional reaction, you'll be tentative in your sales to non-Americans and if the buyer does explode with anger at one of your proposals, you tend to overreact. Instead, you should merely see it as a negotiating ploy that might be perfectly acceptable in their culture.

**You tend to expect short-term profits.** Besides wanting to conclude the negotiations before you have built a relationship with the other side, you also expect quick results from the deal that you cut. Realize that you look at quarterly dividends, where foreign investors are looking at 10-year plans. To many non-Americans this comes across, unfairly I think, as a "fast-buck" mentality. Where they are looking to build a long-term relationship, you appear to concentrate only on profits, and this can be offensive to them.

**You are less likely to speak a foreign language.** There's no question that English is now the business language of the world. Conferences in Europe are typically conducted in English these days because it is the common-denominator language. Most European businesspeople can speak two foreign languages and one of them is always English. Most Asian businesspeople can at least understand English even if they cannot speak it well. Sadly, hardly any Americans can speak German or Japanese. If you do know a foreign language, it is probably Spanish or French.

To realize how arrogant this may appear to non-Americans you have only to think of how frustrated you became when you first dined in a Parisian restaurant. When the waiter didn't appear to speak any English, you probably thought as I did, "This is a tourist restaurant. They must get English-speaking people in here all the time. Why is he being so difficult by refusing to speak English?" Unfortunately, this attitude is all too prevalent with American businesspeople. Any expectation that "If they want to do business with us they should learn our language," can come across as irritatingly arrogant to a foreigner. Instead, you should always appear surprised and delighted that they speak even a few words of our language. You should always make an effort to speak a few words of their language even if it's only to say good morning and thank you.

**You are probably uncomfortable with silence.** Fifteen seconds of silence to you seems like an eternity. Do you remember the last time the sound went out on your television? You were probably thumping the top of the set within 15 seconds.

Particularly to Asians who are comfortable with long periods of meditation, this impatience appears to be a weakness, and a weakness that they can exploit. When dealing with non-Americans, don't be intimidated by long periods of silence. Instead, see it as a challenge to not be the next one to talk. After an extended period of silence, the next person to talk loses because that person will make a concession.

A student of mine, who is an investment banker, told me about negotiating a mortgage loan worth tens of millions of dollars with inventors in Shanghai, China. "There were 23 of us seated around the conference table," he told me. "Suddenly they all shut up and went into total silence. Fortunately, I remembered what you told me and glanced at my watch, determined that I would not be the next one to talk. Twenty-three minutes of excruciating silence went by until finally one of them gave in and broke the silence. From that point we quickly went on to put the deal together."

**You hate to admit that you don't know.** As I will tell you in our next chapter, when we talk about the importance of gathering information, you probably hate to admit that you don't know. Again, this is something that non-Americans know and can use to their advantage. You don't have to answer every question. You are perfectly entitled to say, "That's privileged information at this stage." Or simply tell them that you don't know, or are not permitted to release the information they seek. Not every question deserves an answer.

**You probably feel obligated if they give you a gift.** You will often be overwhelmed with hospitality and gifts by the non-Americans with whom you'll be negotiating. This is an overt attempt to win your favor and you must deal with it. Rather than giving offense by refusing their favors, the best plan is to reciprocate, which eliminates the personal obligation that may have been created. If they take you out to dinner, you should take them to an equally expensive place. It eliminates the obligation, and you have twice the fun.

Finally, permit me to do a little flag-waving here. People around the world still admire and respect Americans and particularly American businesspeople. They trust us and see us as straightforward in our business dealings. So, please don't feel that I have been pointing out the shortcomings of Americans when we deal with non-Americans. I have been teaching you why foreign negotiators often misunderstand Americans. Fair enough?

In the next chapter, I'll teach you how to use pressure points to get what you want and how to protect yourself when the buyer uses them on you.

# Chapter 32

# Negotiating Pressure Points

Louis Armstrong used to tell this story about his early days as a musician: "One night this big, bad-mouth hood crashes my dressing room in Chicago and instructs me that I will open in such-and-such a club in New York the next night. I tell him I got this Chicago engagement and don't plan no traveling. And I turn my back on him to show I'm so cool. Then I hear this sound: SNAP! CLICK! I turn around and he has pulled this vast revolver on me and cocked it. It looks like a cannon and sound like death! So, I look down at that steel and say, 'Weelllll, maybe I do open in New York tomorrow.'"

I've always thought that pulling a gun on someone during negotiations is terribly impolite, so I'm glad there's no need to do it. There are pressure points you can use on the other side that are just as effective and far more acceptable. I'm going to teach you how to use three pressure points on the buyer, and how to defend yourself if the buyer tries to use them on you. In a good negotiation, each side applies pressure very subtly and often the other side is well aware of the pressure that's being used—no threats are made nor is there any trickery involved.

## First Pressure Point: Time Pressure

Under the pressure of time people become more flexible. Under time pressure people make concessions that they wouldn't otherwise make. Your children know this, don't they? When does your child ask you for something? Just as you're rushing out the door, right? When my son John was younger, he would give me a ride to Los Angeles Airport, which is about an hour's drive from my home in La Habra Heights. We wouldn't talk about anything of consequence on the way over there but when we were curbside and the sky cap had my luggage on the cart and I'm about to race off to see if I can catch the plane, he would suddenly say, "Dad, I'm sorry I forgot. I need $50 to fix the muffler on my car."

I would say, "John, don't do this to me. I teach this stuff! How come this didn't come up before?"

He'd tell me, "I'm sorry I forgot, Dad, but I've gotten a fix-it ticket and I have to get it fixed before you get back from your speaking tour. So, please! Can I have the money now and I'll tell you about it next weekend?"

During all those years of dealing with adults, children have learned instinctively that under time pressure, people become more flexible.

The rule in negotiating is that 80 percent of the concessions come down in the last 20 percent of the time available to negotiate. If demands are presented early in a negotiation, neither side may be willing to make concessions, and the entire transaction might fall apart. If, on the other hand, additional demands or problems surface in the last 20 percent of the time available to negotiate, both sides are more willing to make concessions.

Think of the last time that you bought a piece of real estate. It probably took about 10 weeks from the time you signed the initial contract to the time you became the owner of the property. Now think of the concessions that each side made. Isn't it true that during the last two weeks, when things came up to be renegotiated, both sides became more flexible?

Some buyers are unethical enough to use this pressure point against you. They wait until the last minute to bring up elements of the negotiation that they could have brought up earlier and resolved simply. Then when you're getting ready to finalize the arrangements, the buyer puts these problems on the table because he or she knows that you'll be more flexible under time pressure.

One thing this teaches you is that you should tie up all the details up front. Don't leave anything to, "Oh well, we can work that out later," because a matter that appears to be of little importance up front, can become a very big problem under time pressure. You may ask the buyer, "Will you need bar code packaging on these?" The buyer dismisses the question with a wave of his hand saying, "That's not a big problem. We can work that out later." Well it may not be a big problem now, but it could become a big problem later when you're under time pressure to get the order shipped. Why expose yourself to that kind of problem? Tie up all the details up front. When the other side says to you, "We can work that out later, it's not going to be a big problem," bells should start to ring, and lights should start to flash. Don't let the buyer do that to you.

When you're negotiating you should never reveal that you have a deadline. Let's say for example, that you sell institutional furniture and have flown to Dallas to close a sale with a hotel developer. You have a return flight at 6 o'clock. You're eager to catch that flight—but don't let the buyer know. If he does know you have a 6 o'clock flight be sure to let him know you also have a 9 o'clock back up flight, or for that matter you can stay over for as long as it takes to work out a mutually satisfactory arrangement. Because if he knows you're under time pressure he could delay the bulk of the negotiations until the last possible minute. Then there's a real danger that you'll give things away under that kind of time pressure.

In my Power Sales Negotiating seminars, I set up exercises so the students can practice negotiating. They may have 15 minutes to complete a negotiation and I impress on them the importance of reaching agreement within that time. As I walk around the room eavesdropping on the progress of the negotiations, I can tell that during the first 12 minutes, they have trouble making any progress. Both sides are stonewalling the issues and there is very little give and take. At 12 minutes, with 80 percent of the time used up, I take the microphone and tell them they have only three minutes left.

Then I continue periodic announcements to keep the time pressure on them and end with a countdown of the seconds from five to zero. It's clear to see that they make 80 percent of the concessions in the last 20 percent of the time available to negotiate.

An interesting question is raised when both sides are approaching the same time deadline. Let's say that you're a distributor of restaurant equipment. You maintain a showroom attached to your warehouse and have a suite of offices at the same location. Let's say that your five-year lease is up in six months and you must negotiate a renewal with your landlord. You might think to yourself, "I'll use time pressure on the landlord to get the best deal. I'll wait until the last moment to negotiate with him. That will put him under a great deal of time pressure. He'll know that if I move out the place will be vacant for several months until he can find a new tenant." That seems like a great strategy until you realize that there's no difference between that and the landlord refusing to negotiate until the last minute to put time pressure on you.

So, there you have a situation where both sides are approaching the same time deadline. So, which side should use time pressure and which side should avoid it? The answer is that the side who has the most power could use time pressure, but the side with the least power should avoid time pressure and negotiate well ahead of the deadline. Fair enough, but who has the most power? The side with the most options has the most power. If you can't reach a negotiated renewal of the lease, who has the best available alternatives?

To determine this you might take a sheet of paper and draw a line down the middle. On the left side, you list your options if you're unable to renew the lease. What other locations are available to you? Would they cost more or less? How much would it cost you to move the telephones and print new stationery? Would your customers be able to find you if you move?

On the right hand side of the page, you list the landlord's options. How specialized is this building? How hard would it be for him to find a new tenant? Would they pay more or would he have to rent it for less? How much would he have to spend on improvements or remodeling to satisfy a new tenant?

Now you must do one more thing. You must compensate for the fact that whichever side of the negotiating table you're on, you always think you have the weaker hand. After all, you know all about the pressure that's on you, but you don't know about the pressure that's on the landlord. One of the things that makes you a more powerful negotiator is understanding that you always think you have the weaker hand and learning to compensate for that. So, when you list each side's alternatives in this way, you'll probably end up with the conclusion that the landlord has more alternatives than you do. So, compensate for that. But if you do, and clearly the property owner still has more alternatives than you do, then he is the one who has the power. You should avoid time pressure and negotiate the lease renewal with plenty of time to spare.

However, if clearly you have more alternatives available to you than the landlord does, you're able to put him under time pressure by negotiating at the last moment.

Here's another aspect of time pressure: The longer you can keep the other side involved in the negotiation, the more likely they are to move around to your point of view. The next time you're with a buyer and you're beginning to think that you'll never budge him, think of the tugboats in the Hudson River off Manhattan. Remember the Tugboat Close that I taught you in Chapter 27? That tiny tugboat can move that huge ocean liner around if it does it a little bit at a time. However, if the tugboat captain were to back off, rev up its engines and try to force the ocean liner around, it wouldn't do any good. Some people negotiate like that. They reach an impasse in the negotiations that frustrates them. Then they get impatient and try to force the other side to change. Think of that tugboat instead. A little bit at a time it can move the liner around. If you have enough patience, you can change anybody's mind a little bit at a time.

Unfortunately, this works both ways. The longer you spend in a negotiation the more likely *you* are to make concessions. You may have flown to San Francisco to negotiate a large sale. At 8 o'clock the next morning, you're in the office feeling bright, fresh, and determined to hang in and accomplish all of your goals. Unfortunately, it doesn't go as well as you hoped. The morning drags on without any progress so you break for lunch. Then the afternoon passes and you've only reached agreement on a few minor points. You call the airline and re-schedule for the midnight red-eye flight. You break for supper and come back determined to get something done. Look out! Unless you're very careful, by 10 o'clock you'll start making concessions that you never intended to make when you started that morning.

Why does it work that way? Because your subconscious mind is now screaming at you, "You can't walk away from this empty handed after all the time and effort you've spent on it. You have to be able to put something together." Any time you pass the point where you're prepared to walk away, you have set yourself up to lose in the negotiations. A Power Sales Negotiator knows to disregard any time or money that he or she has invested in a project up to any given point. The time and money are gone whether you strike a deal or not. Always look at the terms of a negotiation as they exist at any point and think, "Disregarding all the time and money we've poured into this deal up to now, should we go ahead?" Never be reluctant to pull the plug if it doesn't make sense any more. It's much cheaper to write off your investment than it is to plow ahead with a deal that isn't right for you just because you have so much invested in it. That's one of the things that makes Donald Trump such a powerful negotiator—he's not afraid to pull the plug on a deal that no longer makes sense. He spent $100 million dollars to acquire the site for Television City on the west side of Manhattan. He spent millions more designing plans for the project that would include a 150-story tower (the world's tallest) and a magnificent television studio to which he hoped to attract NBC. However, when he couldn't negotiate the right tax concessions from the city, he shelved the entire project. You have to look at a negotiation in the same way. Forget what you've already invested and examine if it stills looks good the way things stand now.

## Second Pressure Point: Information Power

The side that has the most information can often dominate the other side. Why do countries send spies into other countries? Why do professional football teams study the replays of their opponent's games? Because knowledge is power and the more knowledge one side is able to accumulate about the other, the better chance there is for victory. It works the same way for two salespeople who are vying for an account—the salesperson who knows more about the company and its people stands a better chance making the sale.

I teach a Power Negotiating class for the American College of Physician Executives. This is a wonderful organization, based in Tampa, that specializes in teaching physicians the business side of the healthcare industry. One of my students who managed a large medical group in Florida told me about being approached by a new HMO who wanted to contract with his group for medical services. He was determined to learn all he could about the organization before he went into the negotiations. He discovered a very interesting thing about them. He found that they had been licensed by the state for more than 11 months, but had yet to start operating. They had to start operating in the state before 12 months was up or they would have to reapply for the license. They would be back to square one. The state considered that they met the qualification of operating in the state on the day that they ran their first advertisement. But they couldn't run their first advertisement until they had contracted with a medical provider.

My student used this knowledge to great advantage. He stalled the negotiations until the last week of their year. They had to advertise on Friday of that week or lose their license. On Monday and Tuesday, they placed frantic phone calls to him that he didn't return. By Wednesday, they were willing to concede everything my student wanted. I'm not defending the ethics involved here. I'm just trying to teach you that information gives you power in a negotiation. Always try to know more about the other side than they know about you.

Despite the obvious importance of information in a negotiation, few people spend much time analyzing the other side before starting a negotiation. Even people who wouldn't dream of skiing or scuba diving without taking lessons will jump into a negotiation that could cost them thousands of dollars without spending adequate time gathering the information they should have.

**Rule One for gathering information:** *Don't be afraid to admit that you don't know.* In my seminars I have the students break up into teams of negotiators with some assigned as buyers and others as sellers. I give them enough information to complete a successful negotiation. In fact, I purposely give each side discoverable strengths and weaknesses. I tell each side that if they are asked a question to which they have been given an answer, they may not lie. If they unearth only half of these carefully planted tidbits of information, they would be in a powerful position to complete a successful negotiation.

Unfortunately, no matter how many times I drill students on the importance of gathering information even to the point of assigning 10 minutes of the negotiation for only that, they are still reluctant to do a thorough job.

Why are people reluctant to gather information? Because to find things out, you have to admit that you don't know and most of us are extraordinarily reluctant to admit that we don't know. Let me give you a quick exercise to prove this point.

First, I need you to cover the answers that follow the questions on page 188.

I'm going to ask you six questions, all of which you could answer with a number, but instead of having you try to guess the right number, I'll make it easier for you by asking you for a range. So, if I asked you how many states there are, instead of saying 50, you'd say, "Between 49 and 51." If I asked you how many miles it is from Los Angeles to New York, you might be less sure, so you'd say, "Between 2,000 and 4,000." You could say from one to a million and be 100 percent sure of course, but I want you to be 90 percent sure that the answer falls within the range you give. Do you have the idea?

## Here are the questions:

1. How many counties are there in the United States? (Don't forget to answer with a range.)
2. How many wives did Brigham Young have?
3. How much did we pay Spain for Florida in 1819?
4. How many Perry Mason novels did Erle Stanley Gardner write?
5. How many head of cattle are there in the United States?
6. What was the length of Noah's Ark according to Genesis?

## Here are the answers:

1. There are 3,042 counties in the United States.
2. Brigham Young, the Mormon leader, had 27 wives.
3. We paid $5 million for Florida.
4. Erle Stanley Gardner wrote 75 Perry Mason novels.
5. There are just over 99 million head of cattle in the United States.
6. Noah's Ark was 450 feet long. According to Genesis 6:15, the ark was 300 x 50 x 30 cubits and a cubit equals 18 inches.

Note that all the questions were obscure. There wasn't a reason in the world for you to know the answer to any of them. By rights, you should have heard the questions and thought, "This is ridiculous! I have no idea." However, you probably went ahead and answered them anyway, because we hate to admit that we don't know. So, how did you do? Did you get them all right? Probably not, but think how easy it would have been to get them all right. All you would have had to do is to admit that you didn't know and make the range of your answer huge. You probably didn't do that because just like everyone else, you don't like to admit that you don't know.

So, the first rule for gathering information is: Don't be over-confident. Admit that you don't know and admit that anything you do know may be wrong.

**Rule Two for gathering information:** *Don't be afraid to ask the question.* I used to be afraid to ask questions for fear that it would upset the other person. I was one of those people who say, "Would you mind if I asked you?" or "Would you be embarrassed to tell me?" I don't do that any more. I ask them, "How much money did you make last year?" If they don't want to tell me, they won't. However, even if they don't answer the question I'll still be gathering information. Just before General Schwarzkopf sent our troops into Kuwait, Sam Donaldson asked him, "General, when are you going to start the land war?"

Did he really think that the general was going to say, "Sam, I kind of promised the president that I wouldn't tell any of the 500 reporters that keep asking me that question, but because you asked I'll tell you: At 2 a.m. on Tuesday we're going in"? Of course, Schwarzkopf wasn't going to answer that question, but a good reporter asks the question anyway. It might put pressure on the other person or annoy them so that they blurt out something they didn't intend to. Just judging the other person's reaction to the question might tell you a great deal.

As I travel around the country, I'm always looking for bargains in real estate. Several years ago I was in Tampa and noticed a "For Sale by Owner" classified advertisement that offered a waterfront home on an acre of land for $120,000. To someone who lives in Southern California, as I do, it seemed like an incredible bargain. If you could find an acre of waterfront land here, it would sell for many millions. So, I called the owner to get more information. He described the property and it sounded even better. Then I said, "How long have you owned it?" That's a normal question that very few people would have trouble asking. He told me that he'd owned it for three years. Then I asked, "How much did you pay for it?" That's a question that many people would have trouble asking because they might think it would upset the other person and make them angry. There was a long pause on the other end of the line. Finally, he responded, "Well, all right, I'll tell you. I paid $85,000." Immediately I knew that this wasn't the great deal that it appeared to be. It had been a very flat real estate market in Tampa and he hadn't improved the property. So, I learned a great deal from asking that one question. However, what if he had refused to answer the question, if he had told me that it wasn't any of my business what he paid for it, would I still have been gathering information? Of course, I would. What if he'd lied to me? What if he'd said, "Let's see what did we pay for it? Oh, yes, we paid $200,000. We're really losing money." If he'd have lied to me like that, would I still be gathering information? Of course. So, don't be afraid to ask the question.

Telling you that one way to get information is to ask may seem incredibly simplistic to you, but all too often salespeople don't ask because they're afraid to or because they think they know the answer already. I once spoke at a banquet for a large packaging company and sat at dinner between a sales manager of the packaging company and the vice president of a food manufacturing company who was the packaging company's largest customer. I was curious to know how much of the food company's business went to this packaging company so I leaned over to the sales manager of the packaging company and asked, "How much of their business does this company give you?"

He told me, "We don't know. They would never reveal that, but we do know they like to spread their business around."

A little later I leaned over to the vice president of the food company and asked, "How much of your packaging business do you give this company?"

He said, "Twenty-seven point eight percent."

Surprised that he had told me, I said, "I suppose you like to spread your business around?"

He replied, "We used to feel that way but now if we find a supplier that will get into bed with us, we'll give them all our business." Here was valuable information that the man on my left would have loved to have known, but he had never asked because he didn't think the man on my right would answer. What does this tell you? *Ask* even if you don't think they'll answer and even if you think you already know the answer.

**Rule Three for gathering information:** *Where you do the asking can make a big difference.* If you meet with the buyer at her corporate headquarters, surrounded by her trappings of power and authority, it's the least likely place for you to get information.

Invisible chains of protocol—what they feel they should be talking about, and what they feel they shouldn't, always surround people in their work environment. When people are in their work environment, they're cautious about sharing information. Get them away from their work environment, and information flows much more freely. I'm sure you agree that if you could get the buyer out to dinner or to play golf, she'd tell you all kinds of things that she wouldn't tell you in her office. Fortunately, it doesn't take that much. Sometimes all that it takes is to get that buyer down the hall to the company lunchroom for a cup of coffee. Often that's all it takes to relax the tensions of the negotiation and get information flowing.

Apart from directly asking the buyer, how else can you gather information about a company? Well, one thing you can do is ask people who have done business with them already. I think you'll be amazed—even if you thought of them as competition—how much they're willing to share with you. So, find out who else they do business with and call that salesperson.

Another great idea is to ask people further down the corporate ladder than the person with whom you plan to deal. Let's say you're going to be negotiating with someone at the main office of a chain of computer warehouse stores. You might call up one of the branch offices and get an appointment to stop by and see the local manager. Do some preliminary negotiating with that person. He'll tell you a lot (even though he can't actually negotiate the deal) about how the company makes decisions, why they select one vendor over another, the specification factors they consider, the profit margins they expect, the way they normally pay, and so on. Be sure that you're "reading between the lines" in that kind of conversation. Without your knowing it, the negotiations may have already begun. For example, the branch manager may tell you, "They never work with less than 20-percent profit margins," when that may not be the case at all. And never tell the branch manager anything you wouldn't want him to tell the people at the head office. Take the precaution of assuming anything you say will get back to people higher up.

**Rule Four for gathering information:** *Go through peer groups because people have a natural tendency to share information with their peers.* At a cocktail party, you'll find attorneys talking about their cases to other attorneys, when they wouldn't consider it ethical to share that information with anyone outside their industry. Doctors will talk about their patients to other doctors, but not outside their profession.

Power Sales Negotiators know how to use this phenomenon, because it applies to all occupations, not just in the professions. Engineers, controllers, foremen, and truck drivers all have allegiances to their occupations, as well as their employers. Put them together with each other, and information will flow that you couldn't get any other way.

You can take an engineer from your company with you and let your engineer mix with their engineers. You'll find out that unlike top management—the level at which you may be negotiating—engineers have a common bond that spreads throughout their profession, rather than just a vertical loyalty to the company for which they currently work. So, all kinds of information will pass between these two.

Naturally, you have to watch out that the person you bring along doesn't give away information that could be damaging to you. So, be sure you pick the right person. Caution her carefully on what you're willing to tell the other side, and what you're not willing to tell: your open agenda and your hidden agenda. Then let her go to it, trying to gather information. Peer group information gathering is very effective.

**Rule Five for gathering information:** *We tend to give more weight to information that we gain surreptitiously.* Always consider that the information could have been planted to fool or distract you.

One of my pupils is Andy Mills, the president of Medline Industries, Inc., a billion-dollar hospital supply company. Andy not only has me train his huge sales force but he has studied my material so well that he could go out and do my seminars for me. He loves to negotiate, and particularly with me. Once we got a check from his company for a seminar that I did, and written on the stub was a note to his assistant that said, "Roger charges too much. Use him if we have more than 30 people in the class, but use the other training company for smaller groups." My assistant brought it to me concerned that we were going to lose all his business. "Don't worry about it," I told her. "That's just Andy. He knows that we tend to give more weight to information that we thought we weren't supposed to read."

# Third Pressure Point: Being Prepared To Walk Away

The last of the three pressure points is the most powerful. It's projecting to the buyer that you will walk away from the negotiations if you can't get what you want. In fact, if there's one thing that I can impress upon you that would make you a 10 times better negotiator, it's this: Learn to develop walk-away power. The danger is that there's a mental point that you pass when you will no longer walk away. There's a point you reach in the negotiations when you start thinking: I'm going to make this sale. I'm going to get the best price and the best terms I possibly can, but I have to nail this one down.

The minute you pass the point when you'll willing to say, "I'm prepared to walk away from this," you lose in the negotiations. So, be sure you don't pass that point. There's no such thing as a sale you have to make at any price. The minute you pass the point when you think there is, you've lost in the negotiations.

At seminars when people come up to me and tell me that they made a mistake in negotiations, this is always a part of the problem. They passed the point where they were prepared to walk away. Somewhere down the line in relating the story, they'll say to me, "I made up my mind that I was going to get it, and I know that was the turning point in the negotiations." It was the point at which this person lost.

Many years ago, my daughter bought her first car. She went down to the dealer and test-drove an expensive used car. She fell in love with the car, and they knew it! Then she came back and wanted me to go back down with her, to renegotiate a better price! Tough situation, right? On the way down there, I said, "Julia, are you prepared to come home tonight without the car?"

And she said, "No, I'm not. I want it, I want it!"

So, I told her, "Julia, you might as well get your checkbook out and give them what they're asking. Because you've already set yourself up to lose in the negotiations. We've got to be prepared to walk away."

We walked out of the showroom twice in the two hours that we spent negotiating, and bought the car for $2,000 less than she would have paid for it.

How much money was she making while she was negotiating? She was making a thousand dollars an hour (bearing in mind that I waived my normal fee)! We'd all go to work for a thousand dollars an hour, wouldn't we? You can't make money faster than you can when you're negotiating.

So, you become a Power Sales Negotiator when you learn to project to the other side that you will walk away if you can't get what you want.

Be sure that you've built enough desire before you threaten to walk away. Obviously, if the person doesn't particularly want your product or service yet, and you threaten to walk away, you're going to find yourself standing on the sidewalk saying, "What happened?"

You should consider selling as a four-step process:

1. **Prospecting.** Looking for people who want to do business with you.

2. **Qualifying.** Can they afford to do business with you?

3. **Desire-building.** Making them want your product or service above everybody else's.

4. **Closing; getting the decision.** Walking away is a Stage-Four Gambit. You use it after you've built desire and you're going for the decision.

Please remember that the objective is to get what you want by threatening to walk away. The objective is not to walk away. Don't call me to say, "Roger, you'd be so proud of me! I just walked away from a million-dollar sale!" It's like General Patton saying to his troops, "Keep the objective clear. The objective is not for you to die for your country. It's for you to get the other side to die for their country."

In a heavy situation, when there's a big sale at stake, don't threaten to walk away without the protection of Good Guy/Bad Guy. Don't do it alone. You should have a Good Guy left behind. Then, if you threaten to walk away and they don't say, "Hey, wait a minute, where are you going? Come on back, we can still put this together," you still have the Good Guy left behind who can say, "Look. He's just upset right now. I think we can still put this together, if you can be a little bit more flexible in your pricing."

Power Sales Negotiators know that learning to subtly communicate to the other side that you're prepared to walk away is the most powerful pressure point of them all.

In this chapter you've learned about the three major pressure points in a negotiation: Time Pressure, Information Power, and Walk-Away Power. In our next chapter, I'll tell you what to do when problems arise in a negotiation.

# Chapter 33

# Handling Problem Negotiations

If you're a big-ticket salesperson, you will frequently encounter **impasses, stalemates, and deadlocks** in your negotiations with buyers. Here's how I define the three terms:

1. An **Impasse** is when you disagree on a major issue and it threatens the negotiations.

2. A **Stalemate** is when you and the buyer are still talking but you seem unable to make any progress toward a solution.

3. A **Deadlock** is when the lack of progress has frustrated both sides so much that neither you nor the buyer see any point in talking to each other any more.

## Handling an impasse

Remember that an impasse is when you disagree on a major issue and it threatens the negotiations. It's easy for an inexperienced negotiator to confuse an impasse with a deadlock. Let me give you four examples:

1. The purchasing agent at the automobile manufacturer in Detroit says, "You'll have to cut your price by 2 percent a year for the next five years, or we'll have to re-source." You know it's impossible to do that and still make a profit, so it's easy to think you've deadlocked, when you've really only reached an impasse.

2. The buyer says, "I would love to do business with you, but you charge too much. I have three other bids that are way below what you're asking." Your company's firm policy is that they won't let you participate in bid shopping, so it's easy to think you're deadlocked when you've really only reached an impasse.

3. They're yelling at you, "I don't want to talk about it. Take the shipment back and give us credit, or the next person you hear from will be my attorney!" This isn't necessarily a deadlock; it could be only an impasse.

4. The president of a plumbing supply company pokes his cigar in your face and growls, "Let me tell you the facts of life, buddy boy. Your competition will give me 90 days' credit, so if you won't do that, we don't have anything to talk about." You know that your company hasn't made an exception to their 30-days-net rule in the 72 years they've been in business, so it's easy to think you're deadlocked, when you've really only reached an impasse.

All of these may sound like deadlocks to the inexperienced negotiator, but to the Power Sales Negotiator, they're only impasses. You can use a very easy gambit whenever you reach an impasse. It's called the Set-Aside Gambit and it involves getting the other side to set aside the impasse issue and discuss minor issues first. By building momentum as you resolve the minor issues, you'll find that the impasse issue is far more resolvable than it appeared to be at first.

In 1991, Secretary of State James Baker used the Set-Aside Gambit very effectively when he was faced with an intransigent Israel as he tried to get them to the peace table with the PLO. They felt that any compromise would require them to give up territory, and they didn't want to give credence to that idea by talking about it to their enemy. James Baker was a good enough negotiator to know that he should set aside the impasse issue and create momentum on minor issues. So, he said in effect, "Fine, we realize that you're not ready for peace talks yet, but let's just set that issue aside for a moment. If we did have peace talks, where should we have them? Would it make more sense to do it in Washington, or the Middle East, or perhaps a neutral city such as Madrid?" He inched the negotiations forward by talking about that for a while. Then he raised the issue of PLO representation at the talks. If the PLO were represented at the talks, who would be acceptable representatives from the PLO? After he had created momentum on these minor issues, he found it much easier to get the Israelis to agree to meet with and finally recognize the Palestine Liberation Organization.

Haven't you had a buyer present something that forcefully with you? "We might talk about doing business with you, but we would absolutely never, ever go along with these payment terms. If that's what you want, forget it. You get paid in 90 days just like all of our other suppliers. If you can live with that, we'll talk. If you can't, we don't have anything to talk about."

The Set-Aside Gambit is what you should use when you're talking to a buyer and they say to you, "We might be interested in talking to you, but we have to have a prototype from you by the first of the month for our annual sales meeting in New Orleans. If you can't move that quickly, let's not waste time even talking about it."

Even if it's virtually impossible for you to move that quickly, you still use the Set-Aside Gambit: "I understand exactly how important that is to you, but let's just set that aside for a minute and talk about the other issues. Tell me about the specs on the job. Do you require us to use union labor? What kind of payment terms are we talking about?"

When you use the Set-Aside Gambit, you resolve many of the little issues first to establish some momentum in the negotiation, before leading up to the big issues. As I'll teach you in Chapter 37 on win-win negotiating, you don't want to narrow it down to just one issue (because with only one issue on the table, there has to be a winner and there has to be loser). However, by resolving the little issues first, you create momentum that will make the big issues much easier to resolve. Inexperienced negotiators always seem to think that they need to resolve the big issues first. "If we can't get together on the major things like price and terms, why waste much time talking to them about the little issues?" Power Sales Negotiators understand the other side will become much more flexible after you've reached agreement on the small issues.

## Key points to remember about handling an impasse

➢ Don't confuse an impasse with a deadlock. True deadlocks are very rare, so you've probably only reached an impasse.

> ➤ Handle an impasse with the Set-Aside Gambit: "Let's just set that aside for a moment and talk about some of the other issues, may we?"
> ➤ Create momentum by resolving minor issues first, but don't narrow the negotiation down to only one issue. For more on this read Chapter 37 on win-win negotiating.

## Handling a stalemate

Somewhere between an impasse and a deadlock, you'll sometimes encounter a stalemate. That's when both sides are still talking but seem unable to make any progress toward a solution.

Being in a stalemate is similar to being "in irons," which is a sailing expression meaning that the boat has stalled with its head into the wind. When you tack, which means to turn the boat across a head wind, you must do it with a smooth, continuous motion or the boat will get stuck with its bow into the wind. No sailboat will sail directly into the wind, only at an angle to the wind. If you lose momentum as you tack there is not enough crosswind to move the bow of the boat around. So, if you go "into irons" you must try different things to get the boat to move. You may be able to do it by waggling the tiller or wheel, or you may have to reset the sails to change the dynamics and correct the problem. Similarly, when negotiations stalemate you must change the dynamics to re-establish momentum. Here are seven things that you can do, other than lowering your price:

1. Change the venue by suggesting that you continue the discussion over lunch or dinner.
2. Ease the tension by talking about hobbies, or a piece of gossip that's in the news, or by telling a funny story.
3. Explore the possibility of a change in finances, such as extended credit, a reduced deposit with the order, or restructured payments. Any of these may be enough to change the dynamics and move you out of the stalemate. Remember that the other side may be reluctant to raise these issues for fear of appearing to be in poor financial condition.
4. Discuss methods of sharing the risk with the other side. Taking on a commitment that may turn sour might concern them. Try suggesting that a year from now you'll take back

any unused inventory in good condition, for a 20-percent re-stocking fee. Perhaps a weasel clause in the contract, that applies should the market change, will assuage their fears.

5. Try changing the ambiance in the negotiating room. If the negotiations have been in a low key Attitudinal Drive, try moving into a Competitive Drive. If the negotiations have been in a Competitive Drive, try switching to more of an Attitudinal Drive. Re-read Chapter 29 about different negotiating drives and consider how you could switch the stalled negotiations from one drive to another.

6. Suggest a change in specifications, packaging, or shipping method to see if this shift will make the buyers think more positively.

7. It may be possible to get them to overlook any difference of opinion provided you agree to a method of arbitrating any dispute should it become a problem in the future.

If you are team negotiating, you have a couple more options:

1. Change the people in the negotiating team. A favorite expression that attorneys use is, "I have to be in court this afternoon, so my partner Charlie will be taking my place." The court may be a tennis court, but it's a tactful way of changing the team.

2. Remove a member who may have irritated the other side. A sophisticated negotiator won't take offense at being asked to leave because he or she may have played a valuable role as a Bad Guy. Now it's time to alternate the pressure on the other side by making the concession of removing them from your team.

When a sailboat is "in irons" the skipper may not know exactly how to solve the problem. He has to try different things and see what works.

## Key points to remember about handling a stalemate

➢ Be aware of the difference between an impasse, a stalemate, and a deadlock. In a stalemate, both sides are still motivated to find a solution, but neither can see a way to move forward.

➢ The response to a stalemate should be to change the dynamics of the negotiation by altering one of the elements.

# Handling a deadlock

If things get any worse, you may reach a deadlock. This is something that occurs when the lack of progress has frustrated both sides so much that neither you nor the buyer see any point in talking to each other any more. Deadlocks are rare in the sales profession, but if you do reach one, the only way to resolve it is to bring in a third party—someone who will act as a mediator or arbitrator.

There is a major difference between an arbitrator and a mediator. In the case of an arbitrator, both sides agree before the process starts that they will abide by the decision of the arbitrator. If a union vital to the public's welfare goes on strike (such as the union of transportation or sanitation workers) the federal government will eventually insist that an arbitrator be appointed, and both sides must realize that they will have to settle for what the arbitrator thinks is fair. A mediator doesn't have that kind of power. A mediator is someone brought in to facilitate a solution. He or she simply acts as a catalyst, using negotiating skills to seek a solution that both sides will accept as reasonable.

Inexperienced negotiators are reluctant to bring in a mediator because they see their inability to resolve a problem as being failure on their part. "I don't want to ask my sales manager for help because he'll think of me as a poor negotiator," is what is running through this person's mind. Power Sales Negotiators know that there are many reasons why a third party can resolve a problem, other than that they are better negotiators. Here are some of the reasons:

1. A mediator can go to both sides separately and suggest to each that he or she take a more reasonable position. An arbitrator can even force this by telling both sides to bring in a final solution within 24 hours, telling them that he or she will pick the more reasonable of the two. This forces each side to be more reasonable because they each fear that the other will present a more attractive plan. It becomes, in effect, a closed-bid auction of ideas.

2. A mediator listens better to each side because he or she does not have to filter the information through a prejudiced position. Because this person has less at stake, he or she may well hear something to which an opponent would be deaf.

3. A mediator can persuade better because both sides perceive this person as having less to gain. As I pointed out in my

Nightingale-Conant program *Secrets of Power Persuasion*, you lose much of your ability to persuade if the listener sees you as having something to gain. For example, buyers will believe you much more readily if you tell them that you're not on commission.

4. When negotiating directly you tend to assume that if the other side floats a trial balloon, then they would be willing to agree to what they're suggesting. A mediator can go to each side and propose a solution without implying that the other side is willing to comply.

5. An arbitrator can get both sides back to the negotiating table without having to promise concessions.

Either an arbitrator or a mediator can be very effective, but only if both sides see the person as reasonably neutral. Sometimes you must go to great lengths to assure this perception. Each side may insist on a team of three arbitrators, so each side selects one, and those two must agree on a third. They should all be members of the American Arbitration Association to assure that they adhere to the highest ethical standards. The Association has strict rules for the way their members can arbitrate and still stay within the law.

As a salesperson, you won't be going to that much trouble. You'll be using a mediator, not an arbitrator, and chances are that your mediator will be your sales manager or someone else from your organization. If you bring in your sales manager to resolve a dispute with a customer, what is the chance that your customer will perceive him or her as neutral? Somewhere between nil and zero, right? So, your sales manager must do something to create a feeling of neutrality in the buyer's mind. The way to do this is for your sales manager to make a small concession to the other side early in the mediation process.

Your sales manager comes in and, even if she's fully aware of the problem, says, "I haven't really had a chance to get into this yet. Why don't you both explain your position and let me see if I can come up with a solution that you can both live with?" The terminology is important here. By asking both sides to explain their positions, she is projecting that she comes to the process without prejudice. Also, note that she's avoiding the use of "we" when she refers to you.

Having patiently heard both sides out, she should then turn to you and say, "Are you being fair pushing that? Perhaps you could give a little on the terms (or some other detail)? Could you live with 60 days?" Don't feel that your sales manager is failing to support you. What's she's trying to do is position herself as neutral in your customer's eyes.

I once helped negotiate the sale of one company to another. We had two teams of attorneys that were working trying to resolve the many differences. After weeks of negotiating, we appeared to reach an absolute deadlock. One of the attorneys resolved the deadlock when he was smart enough to say, "This is obviously going to take more time than I thought. I have to be in court this afternoon, but I'll tell you what, my partner Joe will be in after lunch to take my place."

So, Joe came in after lunch. He was completely new to the situation. Each side had to explain where they were in the negotiations. Joe took great pains to position himself as neutral. He did this by saying to his side, "Are we being fair to them, by pushing that point? Maybe we could give a little bit there."

That caused the other side to think, "Well, he seems much more reasonable than the last person. Maybe we can find a way past this after all." Having positioned himself as neutral, he was able to find common ground in the negotiations that got us past the deadlock.

So, anytime you reach a deadlock in the negotiations, bring in a third party who's perceived as reasonably neutral by the other parties.

That's what President Carter was able to do at Camp David. It took years and years for the United States to position itself as neutral with Egypt. They always saw us as the enemy and the Soviet Union as their friend. Henry Kissinger saw a remarkable opportunity to change all that, and he jumped at it. He was in Anwar El Sadat's office at a time when Sadat was desperately trying to get the Soviets to clear the Suez Canal, which was shut down with the wrecks of ships sunk during the war.

The Soviets were willing to do the job but their bureaucracy stopped them from moving fast enough. Kissinger said, "Would you like us to help you?"

An astonished Sadat said, "You would do that?" Kissinger picked up the phone in Sadat's office and called President Nixon in the White House. Within days, the sixth fleet was on its way to the Suez. With this one act, they started the process of positioning us as reasonably neutral between the Israelis and the Egyptians. An act that eventually led to President Carter's Camp David Accord.

Don't assume that you must avoid impasses, stalemates, and deadlocks at all cost. An experienced negotiator can use them as tools to pressure the other side. Once you feel that a deadlock is unthinkable, it means that you're no longer prepared to walk away, and you have surrendered your most powerful pressure point.

## Key points to remember about handling a deadlock

➢ The only way to resolve a true deadlock is by bringing in a third party.

➢ The third party can act as a mediator or an arbitrator. Mediators can only facilitate a solution, but with an arbitrator, both sides agree up front that they will abide by the arbitrator's final decision. (For an extended explanation of the difference between mediation and arbitration, please refer to my book *Secrets of Power Negotiating, 3rd Edition*, published by Career Press in 2010.)

➢ Don't see having to bring in a third person as a failure on your part. There are many reasons why this person can reach a solution that the parties to the negotiation couldn't reach alone.

➢ The third party must be seen as neutral by both sides.

➢ If the third party is not seen as neutral, he or she should create that appearance by making a small concession to the other side early in the negotiation.

➢ Keep an open mind about the possibility of a deadlock. You can develop your full power as a Power Sales Negotiator only if you're prepared to walk away. By refusing to consider a deadlock, you're giving away a valuable pressure point.

In this chapter, I taught you how to handle problem negotiations. I've taught you how to handle impasses, stalemates, and deadlocks in a negotiation. In the next chapter, I'll deal with a situation that every salesperson dreads.

# Chapter 34

# Handling an Angry Person

Angry customers are a serious problem that you can encounter in sales negotiations. Something has gone dramatically wrong—the shipment was delayed, you accidentally overcharged them, they feel you lied to them—whatever, but the result is that you have furious customers on your hands. Every salesperson dreads this situation.

If you'll learn to go through the three stages that I'm going to teach you now, you will find that frustration over this kind of problem is a thing of the past and you will be able to smoothly resolve the situation.

Several years ago, the mayors of the 442 cities in California asked me to teach them how to handle hostage negotiations. "Let's suppose," I said to them, "that you're the mayor of a small California city, and you've been called into a terrorist situation downtown. There's a man holding a gun on a hostage in one of the buildings. Your police chief is a little to the right of Genghis Khan, so he's in favor of blowing the whole place apart and killing everybody in sight. Somebody hands you a bullhorn, and says: 'Okay, negotiate our way out of this.'"

A mayor called out, "Wait a minute. I only got elected by 47 votes!"

Of course it's unlikely that you as a salesperson will ever be in that kind of a situation, but if you can learn to handle a hostage situation you'll be able to smoothly handle an angry buyer. First, of course, you must let the person dissipate some of the anger. People need to vent. Be sure to do this in a closed office where the ruckus is not disturbing the people around you. As quickly as you can, move to Stage One.

## Stage 1: Establish Criteria

In this stage, you should find out exactly what the other side wants to do. Do this even when you're sure that you won't like what you're about to hear. Even if you cannot, or will not, make any concessions to them at all, find out exactly what it is they want. Get them to establish their criteria.

In the terrorist situation, they might want five minutes on a local radio station. It might be $100,000, or the release of some prisoners. Or it might be something that you're happy to give them. When O.J. Simpson was fleeing police, he surrendered for a glass of orange juice and the chance to use the bathroom. In the siege in Waco, Texas, David Koresh wanted them to broadcast a tape he had recorded. The Unabomber wanted his manifesto published in the *New York Times*.

A nationwide real estate franchise company hired me to talk on Power Sales Negotiating at its annual meeting. As they finished handing out the trophies and broke for lunch, I saw one of the franchise brokers come storming to the front of the room. He grabbed the vice president of the company and yelled, "Well, you did it to me again! One of my top salespeople didn't get a trophy. How am I supposed to keep my sales force motivated if you don't give them recognition?"

He must have caught the vice president at a bad moment because he responded, "You know why he didn't get his trophy? Because you didn't turn in your sales report on time!"

"Yes, I did!"

"No, you didn't. You've been with us for five years now, and you've never turned a sales report in on time yet!" And the fight was on! The people who had lined up to try and talk with the vice president started drifting away in embarrassment, and I started to time this thing to see how long it would take the vice president to find out exactly what the branch manager wanted him to do.

Twenty-three minutes went by. By then, they were in a screaming match. The branch manager was saying, "I'm going to leave the franchise. I'm going to pull all of my salespeople out, and we're leaving!"

And the vice president responded, "If that's all the loyalty we've got from you, we're probably better off without you!"

A major escalation of the problem, when all that it really took was for the vice president to stay calm and say to the branch manager, "Wow, I'm sorry that he didn't get his trophy. What exactly is it you would like me to do?"

The branch manager would have responded, "Give him some recognition during the lunch break or this afternoon, would you?"

Then the vice president could have replied, "If I do that for you, what will you do for me? Can I get your assurance that your sales reports will be in on time in future, so that this could never happen again?" (That's the Trading Off Gambit that I taught you in Chapter 16.) And it all would have been over!

We see that kind of escalation all the time, don't we? You walk into your office and two employees are arguing about something over at the water cooler. They look upset so you go over to see if you can help. When you find out what they're arguing about, you can't believe what a petty matter it is. One of them borrowed the other's stapler and didn't return it, and the whole thing blew up out of proportion. It happens in our personal lives too with our spouses and children. Something is said. The wrong response is made. Soon the whole thing flares up, and we never meant it to get that bad, but we just don't know how to pull back from the positions that we've taken in the negotiation.

So, that's always the first stage in any negotiation: Ask what the other person wants you to do. Sometimes it's not as bad as you might fear. Do you remember the Lufthansa airplane that got hijacked out of Frankfurt, Germany? The passengers thought they were going to get off in Cairo three hours later. Instead, they were hijacked, flown all over Europe and then to New York and back. Finally, the passengers were released. One of them spotted a Lufthansa official and went roaring up to him. He was furious. He had missed all of his business appointments in Cairo and had been terrorized for three days by what he saw as Lufthansa's lack of security. Imagine what must have been going on in this official's mind in terms of what it would take to calm this man down. Fortunately, he knew the rule. Find out what people want first. Do you remember what the passenger wanted? Frequent flyer mileage! That's all that he wanted to resolve the problem.

So, sometimes it's not as bad as you fear, but even if it is, you're better off to get the angry person committed to a position. In response, we let them know what we are prepared, or not prepared, to do. So, in Stage One we Establish Criteria.

# Stage 2: Exchange Information

Having established criteria so that each side understands exactly what the other side is initially willing to do, then you go to Stage Two where you will find out everything you can about the situation.

This is one of the most critical parts of any negotiation, to probe for more information. I taught you in the last chapter how information is one of the critical pressure points. Here we see that it's the second stage of every negotiation.

Find out all you possibly can. Don't jump to conclusions at this stage. Ask for information. In the case of the terrorist situation, we want to know if this person is a member of an organized group. Has he ever followed through on this threat before? What religion is he? Is there a minister or a priest we can call in? Where's his family? Who can we bring in to help us with the situation? We get all the information we possibly can.

Whenever you hear about a hostage negotiation where everything went wrong and people got killed, examine the news reports and see if this wasn't the problem: The negotiators weren't able, or simply didn't have the patience, to find out more about the situation.

One day a man was walking down Rodeo Drive in Beverly Hills with a gun in his pocket. (Now, as you may have heard, this is not an unusual part of living in Southern California. Do you remember when we had the freeway shootings a while back? Overnight we had bumper stickers on our cars that said, "Cover me—I'm changing lanes." So, we're used to this kind of thing.) The man walked into Van Cleef and Arpels, the jewelry store, and pulled the gun out of his pocket. The guard at the front door locked the door of the store with them all inside. Now here's a multiple-choice question for you: Was that a) Dumb, b) Stupid, or c) All of the above. I understand that now they have a sign on the Van Cleef and Arpels lunchroom wall that says, "First you leave the store, then you lock the gunman in."

The Beverly Hills police called out every SWAT team in Southern California. Soon they had a gunman on the rooftop of every building, and had this two-block shopping street completely barricaded off for three whole days. The merchants were going out of their minds. They were losing millions. They were passing the hat, trying to raise bail for this man. On the third day, they finally had this young man in custody and only then, finally, learned his name. They hadn't gone through the information gathering stage.

If you're a sales manager you may have a key employee who's about to quit. What exactly would it take for this person to stay with you? Find out even if you may not like what you're going to hear. Find out even if you have a firm policy against giving people an increase in pay when they threaten to quit. Instead of becoming enraged, Exchange Information.

Having done that, you may be in a position to say, "Charlie, we've been friends for six years! I can't believe that you'd take the risk of working for another company for that little extra money!" The more you probe for information, the more things will come to the surface that affect the negotiations. This employee may be having marital problems that seem to demand that he leave town and really the money he makes is not the key issue at all.

Exchanging Information is critical to you, and it's the Second Stage of every negotiation.

## Stage 3: Reach for Compromise

Only when you've completed these two stages do you then go to Stage Three—reaching for compromise—which is what most people think of as negotiating.

To start, look for things that they might see of value, but that you're willing to concede in the negotiation because they're not necessarily of value to you and vice versa.

Don't believe that the concessions that you give have to be equal to the concessions that you're seeking. Remember that the angry person with whom you're dealing is thinking irrationally—you are hopefully thinking rationally. In a hostage situation, for example, the perpetrator may be willing to release six hostages in return for a chicken sandwich and a bottle of beer. Similarly, that angry buyer may be willing to overlook a serious problem in return for your personal assurance that it will never happen again.

So, the next time you have an angry buyer on your hands, go through these three stages. See how simply you can calm him down and regain his trust.

In the following section, I'll teach the importance of understanding the other negotiator.

# Understanding the Other Negotiator

# Chapter 35

# Developing Personal Power

Whenever you're in front of a buyer, you develop a feeling about how much power you have over this person. Sometimes it's a mild feeling of confidence that you can make the sale. "I feel lucky today," you may be thinking. Sometimes it's much stronger and you feel that you have *all* the power and are sure that you can make the sale and not have to make any concessions to get it. Perhaps this is an objective feeling—you feel confident because you know that the buyer needs what you have. More often in sales, it's subjective—you feel it but you don't know why you feel it. In this chapter, I'm going to demystify that feeling. When you've finished reading this chapter, you'll understand where your personal power comes from and you'll understand what buyers are doing to you when they seem able to intimidate you.

## Legitimate Power

The first element of personal power is Legitimate Power. Legitimate Power goes to anybody who has a title because titles influence people. If the title on your business card says "vice president," you already have a head start over someone whose card says "salesperson." When I ran the real estate company, I would let the agents who were farming a territory put Area Manager on their business cards. (Farming means that they had staked out an area of 500 homes and they were knocking on doors and mailing newsletters to those homeowners to establish themselves as an expert in that community.) They told me that having the title Area Manager on their cards made a dramatic difference to the way people accepted them.

So, if you don't have an impressive title on your business card, this may be something that your company should reevaluate. The standard designations for territories are that an area manager reports to a district manager who reports to a regional manager. So regional vice president appears to buyers to be the more impressive title. Occasionally I run into a company that designates titles the other way, and the area manager is in charge of the Western United States. I don't suggest that they change, but because it's traditionally done the other way, Area Manager tends to be a less impressive title than Regional Manager.

So, if you have a title, use it on your business card, your letterhead, and your nameplate because titles do influence people.

Legitimate Power also tells you that people with titles should have buyers come to them if possible, rather than negotiating on their territory where they are surrounded by their trappings of power. For example, if you're taking buyers somewhere, it should always be in your car, because it gives you more control. If you're taking them to lunch, it should be to your choice of restaurant not to their favorite place where they feel in control.

So, use your title but at the same time don't be intimidated by another person's title—some of those titles don't mean a thing. My daughter Julia graduated from the University of Southern California with a degree in business finance and went to work for Dean Witter, the New York stockbrokers, in their huge Beverly Hills office. One day she was talking about becoming a vice president at Dean Witter. I told her, "Julia, you have to set realistic goals in life. That's a huge corporation and it may take you years and years to become a vice president."

She replied, "Oh no, I think I'll be a vice president by the end of the year."

I asked her, "How many vice presidents does Dean Witter have?"

And she said, "I don't know but it must be thousands. We have 35 in this one office."

Dean Witter (now called Morgan Stanley Dean Witter) is a company that understands that titles influence people!

In his book *All You Can Do Is All You Can Do*, A.L. Williams brags that at his company he appointed 100 vice presidents a month. If he just made it a policy to go out and shake hands with every new vice president, that alone would be a full time job. So, don't be intimidated if the person to whom you're selling has a fancy title because it may not mean a thing.

There are other forms of Legitimate Power. Positioning in the market place is a form of Legitimate Power. If you can claim that your company is the biggest, or the smallest, or the oldest, or the newest, you have Legitimate Power. You can claim to be the most global company or you can claim to specialize. You can tell the buyer that you're brand new so you're trying harder or that you've been in the business for 40 years. It really doesn't matter how you position yourself—any kind of positioning gives you Legitimate Power.

## Reward Power

The second element of personal power is Reward Power. Power Sales Negotiators understand that anytime you perceive someone as able to reward you, you have given them the power to intimidate you. If you think that buyer is rewarding you by giving you an order, you've given him the power to intimidate you. This is why you feel more intimidated when you're making a big sale than you do when you're making a small one. The potential reward is greater, so you feel intimidated. Of course, that's entirely subjective, isn't it? When you're first getting started, you may feel that sense of reward over a $1,000-dollar sale. Later, it will take a $100,000 sale to get you excited.

Remember Robin Givens? She was Mike Tyson's wife for about eight months. Weren't they a charming couple? Weren't you proud to be floating around in space with those two? When she was heading out to California to hire a divorce attorney, I'm sure she wasn't thinking that she would be rewarding Marvin Mitchelson by giving him the case. No! She was thinking, "If I could get Marvin Mitchelson, that would be really something, because he's the best in the business. You can't do any better than that." You're the best in the business! The people you deal with can't do any better than you. If you're willing to put your personal reputation and expertise, and the reputation and expertise of your company, on the line to solve buyers' problems, they are not rewarding you—you are rewarding them. Of course you can't push that too far because it quickly becomes arrogance, but don't roll over the other way, thinking that they would be rewarding you by giving you an order. I've heard rumors that some salespeople will actually beg a buyer to give them just a small part of the company's business. Can you believe that? Doesn't it sound like a dog begging for table scraps? When you truly believe that you are rewarding the buyer, not the other way around, you'll feel confident in demanding all of their business.

When the buyer starts using Reward Power on you, recognize it and don't let it intimidate you. Some buyers are absolute masters at using Reward Power. They're asking you for a concession and they just happen to mention that they have a big job coming on line next week, for which you might be in the running. Or you'll be talking to them and they'll talk about their yacht down at the harbor, or their ski cabin up in the mountain. They don't even have to come out and tell you that if you did business together you'd get to use them; it is just implied Reward Power. Don't let it intimidate you, but recognize it for what it is; and don't let it throw you off base in the negotiations.

Once you recognize Reward Power and understand what other people are trying to do to you, their ability to control you with it is diminished and you become a lot more self-confident as a negotiator.

## Coercive Power

The opposite side of Reward is Coercive Power. Anytime you perceive someone as able to punish you, they have power over you. You know how awful you feel when the state trooper pulls you over to the side of the road and he's standing there and can write you, or not write you, a ticket. The penalty may not be very great, but the level of intimidation is very great indeed.

So, anytime you perceive that someone is able to punish you, that person has the power to intimidate you—and one of the strongest punishments we know is the power to embarrass people.

Remember when we talked about the Bracketing Gambit in Chapter 5? I told you that you should make your initial proposal so high that it brackets your real objective. Sometimes that's intimidating for you to do. You simply don't have the courage to make those way-out proposals, because you're afraid the other side will laugh at you. The fear of ridicule stops you from accomplishing many things with your life, and you need to come to grips with it. (In my book *The 13 Secrets of Power Performance* I give you the answer to this—you must figure out what you fear the most and do it.) As with Reward Power, the answer lies in experience. While a new salesperson may fear losing a $1,000 sale, the experienced salesperson will not let the loss of a $100,000 sale intimidate him or her.

New salespeople always have trouble with Reward and Coercive Power. When they first make sales calls they see every buyer as being able to reward them by giving them the order, or punish them by turning them down, or worse yet ridiculing them for what they have proposed. Once they've been at it for a while, they recognize that selling is a numbers game just like anything else. If they're working hard at it and talking to a great number of people, there always will be a high percentage of people who will turn them down. Once they understand that it's a numbers game, their perception that people can reward or punish them goes away, and they become a lot more self-confident in what they're doing.

## Reverent Power

The fourth element of power is Reverent Power. It goes to anybody who has a consistent set of values. An obvious example of this would be a religious leader like the Pope, Billy Graham, or Robert Schuller. Pat Robertson was able to make a serious run at the presidency because he articulated one theme: You can trust me because I have a set of values and I am not going to deviate from those values. John F. Kennedy had Reverent Power. When he talked about the mantle of power passing to a new generation born in this century and when he talked about the new frontier, he was projecting that he believed in something—that he had a consistent set of values.

Bill Clinton does not have Reverent Power. I met him at the White House once and I can tell you that he is a very charismatic and brilliantly intelligent person who is an incredibly hard worker. His problem is that he appears to vacillate on different issues. You never quite know whether he has the courage to stay with an issue if the going gets tough.

Lack of Reverent Power was President Carter's downfall. He was one of the nicest, most moral and ethical presidents we've ever had. Also one of the hardest working men who ever occupied the White House and probably among the most intelligent—he majored in nuclear physics! However, he lost his ability to influence because he appeared to vacillate on different issues. We never knew if he felt strongly enough to follow through if the going got tough.

Take, for example, his handling of the visa for the Shah of Iran. The Shah was living in his beautiful villa on Acapulco Bay. He became seriously ill and requested a visa to come to this country for medical treatment. At first, Carter said no, fearing repercussions in Iran. Then he changed his mind and approved the visa so that he could get cancer treatment in New York. When this created a surge of anti-American protests in Iran, he changed his mind again—and made him move to Panama to take the pressure off the situation.

I don't think Ronald Reagan would have done that. He would have made a decision, one way or the other, and stuck with it. Take, for example, Reagan's decision to deny Yasir Arafat a visa when he was invited to address the general assembly of the United Nations in New York. How would you react if you got voted down 150 to 2 in the United Nations—and one of the two was your vote? Then the United Nations decided to move its entire assembly to Geneva to go around your decision! Wouldn't you think that you'd want to take another look at it? Wouldn't you tend to think, "Maybe I went too far on that one?" No! You make a decision and you stick with it because projecting Reverent Power is the most powerful influencing factor you have going for you.

During George Bush's first few years as president, he was all over the board on his level of consistency, and you could see his popularity ratings move in direct relationship to it. At first, he was very consistent in his opposition to new taxes. "They're going to come down from Capitol Hill," he told us, "and tell me we've got to have new taxes. And I'm going to tell them, 'Watch my lips, no new taxes.' So, they'll go back and talk about it, and they'll come back and say, 'Mr. President, we've got to have new taxes' and I'll say, 'Watch my lips, no new taxes.'" We loved him for it! Then he backed down on that issue, and we hated him for it—his popularity dropped from 45 percent to 8 percent almost overnight.

Then along came the Persian Gulf War. How would you rate him for consistency on his handling of the war? A perfect score, right? Nobody could have been more consistent in the way they handled Saddam Hussein, and we loved him for it! His popularity soared from the 40s up to the 90s.

Then he was faced with the problem of the Kurdish refugees. One day he was saying, "I will not send American troops into the middle of a civil war that's been going on forever." That's great, take a stand, but stick with the stand you've taken. The very next day, he changed his mind and sent troops into Northern Iraq. His approval rating immediately dropped from the 90s down to the 50s.

What clearer proof could we have? Reverent Power, the projection of a consistent set of values, influences people. You like and admire consistent behavior in your customers. They like and admire it in you. If you're willing to take a stand for your principles, especially if it appears you're risking financial loss, it builds trust in the other person, and they love you for it.

For example, you might sell computers, and you have the courage to say to your customers, "Of course you'd like to save money; and I'd favor it too if it were the right thing for you to do—but it isn't. I know that you won't be completely happy unless you get the model with the 40 gigabyte hard drive. So, I'm sorry, but I won't sell you anything less."

They love you for that! Of course, it'll raise a few eyebrows, but if you've done your homework and you're right, you'll have power with that customer. If you back down, how are they going to respect you?

Suppose you had the misfortune of having a heart attack. You wake up on a hospital bed and a doctor tells you that you need triple by-pass heart surgery, and you say, "I think I can get by with a double by-pass."

If he says, "Okay, let's try a double by-pass and see how it works out," how would you feel about him then? Would you let that person come near you with a scalpel? I don't think so!

When you project Reverent Power, buyers notice it; they admire and respect the consistent set of values and it gives you influence over them. When you're negotiating with a buyer and you indicate a willingness to cut corners, or in some way pull some strings that you shouldn't be pulling, you may get a short-term gain in your ability to make that sale. However, you get a long-term loss in your ability to influence that buyer over a long period.

Be careful that you're not setting up standards and then breaking your own standards. Don't tell that buyer that you would never cut prices and then go ahead and do it. That's worse than not setting up the standards in the first place. That's what got President Clinton impeached. The consensus of opinion seems to be that he could have gotten away with having consensual sex with an intern if he hadn't so vehemently denied it.

# Charismatic Power

The fifth element of personal power is Charismatic Power—probably the hardest one to analyze and explain. In my book *Secrets of Power Persuasion*, I spend three entire chapters detailing how to develop personal charisma. But for now let's just recognize its power and its limitations.

I'm sure you've had the experience of meeting a celebrity who has an overwhelmingly charismatic personality. When I met President Clinton I was uncomfortable because I'm at the opposite end of the political spectrum and I'm sure he could sense that. I didn't want to say anything that would constitute an endorsement, so I said, "Good luck, Mr. President, don't let them get you down." I didn't think that even Ron and Nancy would have a problem with that. He looked me straight in the eye as he read my name badge and said, "Roger, if you'll stay with me, I'll be there." I said, "I'll be there, Mr. President." Within 15 seconds, he'd gotten a commitment of support from me strictly based on the power of his personality.

Not every president is able to project Charismatic Power. This was Gerald Ford's undoing. He had the other three elements in great abundance, but he didn't have the personality with which to put it across.

Throughout his career, Richard Nixon was dogged by the fact that few people liked him even when they thought he was a brilliant man.

I think that it was George Bush's downfall also, particularly because he followed Ronald Reagan, who was so charismatic. Remember that picture of him during the debate at Williamsburg? He was standing there looking at his watch looking totally bored with the entire process as Clinton leaned into the audience to answer a question.

Salespeople tend to overemphasize Charismatic Power. Many an old-time salesperson has told me, "The only reason my people do business with me is because they like me." Well, not nowadays. Don't fall into the Willie Loman trap. Even 40 years ago, when Arthur Miller wrote *Death of a Salesman* and had Willie Loman saying, "The most important thing is to be liked," he was making fun of it. Sure, that buyer is more likely to give you an order if he or she likes you, but don't think it gives you much control. Buyers are much too sophisticated for that today. It's a long way from control of the negotiations.

Your objective should be to have the buyer like you so much that he will make concessions to you, but not to like the buyer so much that you find yourself making concessions to him.

## Expertise Power

Number six is Expertise Power. When you project to people that you have more expertise than they do in a particular area, you develop power over them. Attorneys and doctors really play this one up, don't they? They develop a whole new language that you can't understand to project to you that they have expertise that you don't have.

There's not a reason in the world why doctors couldn't write prescriptions in English, but if they did, it would take away a little of that mystique, a little of that Expertise Power. Attorneys are the same way. They develop a whole new language that we can't understand so that they project expertise power.

Don't let buyers intimidate you with Expertise Power. Remember when you first started in sales and you studied up on the technical side of what you sold but you weren't confident about it yet? Then you ran into a buyer who appeared to know more about the product than you did. Remember how intimidating that was? Don't let the buyer do it to you. When a buyer questions your expertise don't be afraid to say, "That's not my area of expertise, but our engineers are the finest in the business. You can have complete confidence in them."

## Reverent, Charismatic, Expertise Powers Combined

Let's look at these last three together: Reverent Power, Charismatic Power, and Expertise Power. Power Sales Negotiators know that these three are critical if you are to control the negotiations.

Do you know somebody who doesn't seem to have half the problems that you have when selling buyers on your program? Perhaps you've been out on a sales call with your sales manager and she made it look so easy! She sat down with a buyer and chatted with him for 15 or 20 minutes. She didn't appear to be talking about anything of consequence, but at the end of that time, the buyer was saying to her, "What do we have to do here? Do we need to go with the top of the line or can we get by with the standard? You tell us, you're the expert."

Here's how she got that much power over the buyer: She did a good job of projecting Reverent Power, Charismatic Power, and Expertise Power.

Reverent Power: "I won't do anything that is not in your best interest, regardless of the gain to me." That builds trust, doesn't it?

Charismatic Power: She has a likable personality.

And Expertise Power: Your sales manager projected to the buyer, without it becoming overbearing, that she knew more about it than he did.

When you put these three together, you're very close to having control of the negotiations. You're very close to the point where the buyer will defer the decision: "Well," he'll say, "what do you think we should do?" And he has surrendered control of the negotiation to you.

# Situation Power

The seventh element of personal power is Situation Power. We're all familiar with this one. This is the people down at the post office. Normally very powerless in any other area of life, but in this particular situation they can accept or reject your package; they have power over you and don't they love to use it!

It's prevalent in large organizations or government agencies where the people don't have much latitude in the way they perform their job. When they do get some latitude, when they have some power over you, they're eager to use it.

I remember speaking to a huge sales rally in Halifax, Nova Scotia. The night before I got there, this group had put on the party to end all parties. These people got bombed out of their minds. One of them got undressed to go to bed at 3 o'clock in the morning and then decided he'd like to have some ice in his room. He was standing there in his dazed state, trying to figure out whether it was worthwhile getting some clothes on to go get the ice. Finally he thought, "It's 3 o'clock in the morning. The ice machine's just around the corner from my door. Who's going to see me? I'll slip out the way I am."

Forgetting, of course, that the door would lock behind him the minute he got into the hallway. Soon he's standing outside his door with his bucket of ice and nothing else, mentally debating his options. He finally decided he didn't have too many options, so he set his bucket of ice down and headed on down, across the lobby of the Halifax Sheraton and up to the young woman behind the desk. He asked for another key to his room. She looked straight at him and said, "Sir, before I can give you another key, I need to see some identification." That's Situation Power, and don't they love to use it!

The key issue in negotiating is that sometimes you get to a point where people have so much Situation Power over you that you're going to lose this one, regardless of how good a negotiator you are. So, if you're going to have to make the concession anyway, regardless of what you do, you might as well make the concession as gracefully as you possibly can. It doesn't make any sense to get so upset about it that you lose the goodwill of the other person—and still have to make the concession.

But how many times have we been in a department store to get a refund on something, and the salespeople say to us, "All right, we'll do it this one time, but it's not our normal policy." What sense does that make? If you're going to have to make the concession anyway, you might as well make it as gracefully as you possibly can so that you maintain the goodwill of the other person.

Many years ago when I was a real estate broker, our company built four new homes at one location. In California, we typically build with poured slabs, and just as we finished pouring the slabs, the city building inspector pulled up and walked over. "What are you doing?" he asked casually.

That seemed self-evident to us, but he wasn't known for his sense of humor, so we simply replied, "We're pouring the slabs."

"Not until I've signed off on the plumbing you're not," he said. And we could swear that he was enjoying every minute of this. What followed must have looked like a Keystone Cops routine. Everybody running around trying to find the signed-off building permit card. With growing horror, we realized that he was right. Somebody had goofed, and he had enough Situation Power on us that we were going to have to get a crew of men out there with shovels, digging out the concrete before it set, so that the building inspector could glance at the plumbing, and sign it off.

The point is don't let it upset you. Power Sales Negotiators recognize Situation Power for what it is, pass on, and move into an area where they do have some control.

# Information Power

The final element of personal power is Information Power. Sharing information forms a bond. Withholding information tends to intimidate. Large companies are skillful about doing this. They'll develop a level of information at the executive level that they won't share with the workers. It's not because it's that secretive. It's not because it would do any harm. It's because these large corporations know that a level of secrecy at the executive level gives them control over the workers.

The human race has a tremendous natural desire to know what's going on. We can't stand a mystery. You can put a cow in a field and it will stay in that field all its life and never wonder what's on the other side of that hill. Human beings will spend a billion and a half dollars to throw a Hubbell telescope up in space and another couple of billion to fix it when it doesn't work right because we have to know what's going on out there.

Withholding information can be very intimidating. You've made an extensive presentation to a buying committee and they say to you, "We need to talk about this for a moment. Would you mind waiting outside in the lobby? We'll call you when we're ready for you." Is it any wonder that you feel uncomfortable sitting outside in the lobby? We hate it when people withhold information from us.

The moment we realize they may just be doing this to us as a negotiating gambit, that they may be in there talking about football scores for all we know, they can no longer intimidate us with it. However, they know that by sending us out of the room they have gained psychological advantage. They know that when we walk back into the negotiations, our level of self-confidence has gone down and their level of power has gone up. The moment we realize what they may be doing to us, they can no longer intimidate us with that gambit.

So, these are the eight elements that give you power over the buyer:

1. Legitimate Power: The power of your title or your position in the marketplace.

2. Reward Power: Does he feel that you can reward him, now and in the future?

3. Coercive Power: Does the buyer feel that doing business with you could protect him from problems?

4. Reverent Power: The ability to project a consistent set of values. This builds trust.

5. Charismatic Power: The power of the personality.

6. Expertise Power: Does the buyer believe that you know more about your product than he does?

7. Situation Power: Is the buyer at a disadvantage because of circumstances?

8. Information Power: Does the buyer see you as a storehouse of helpful information?

When you get a chance, take the time to rate yourself in each of those elements. Not as you see yourself, or not even as you really are, but as you think other people see you. How do your buyers perceive you in each of these eight areas? Give yourself a score from 1 to 10 in each area, one being very weak, and 10 being very strong. Add the scores up, which would give you a potential score of 80. If your score comes out in the 60s, that's a very good number for a Power Negotiator. You have power, but you still have empathy for the other side.

If your score is over 70, I'd be a little concerned that you're too intimidating when you're dealing with people.

If your score is less than 60, you have some weak spots. Examine those elements where you gave yourself a low rating and see what you can do to get yourself up to a 10.

As you review this list, remember that these eight power elements are also the ways that buyers can intimidate you into thinking that you don't have any power. So, the next time you're negotiating and you feel that you've lost control—that they're beginning to intimidate you—identify which of those elements is getting to you. Identifying it will help you handle it.

Pay particular attention to the four critical ones for Power Sales Negotiators. The effects of these four together are cataclysmic. When these four come together in one person, it is incredible what happens. The four are:

1. Legitimate Power: The power of the title.

2. Reward Power: The ability to reward people.
3. Reverent Power: The consistent set of values.
4. Charismatic Power: The personality, the pizzazz with which to put it across.

These are powerful whether it's for good or evil. This is what gave Adolph Hitler control of Germany in the 1930s. He kept stressing the title—Fuhrer! Fuhrer! Fuhrer! He kept stressing Reward Power. He kept saying to the German people: If we do this, if we invade Czechoslovakia and Poland, this is what we'll get. The dictatorial Reverent Power—we'll never deviate from this. And he had hypnotic Charismatic Power. He could hold tens of thousands of people mesmerized with his oratory.

It was also the way that David Koresh got control over the Branch Davidians in Waco, Texas. He had so much control over them that they not only wanted him to tell them where to live, what to think, and what to say, but illustrating the ultimate abuse of power: Most of them wanted him to tell them when to die. He was telling his people that he was God. That's a pretty good title—you can't do much better than that! He kept stressing Reward Power: "If you stay with me, you're going to heaven. If you go with them, you're going to jail." Reverent Power: "We don't care what the rest of the world thinks. This is what we believe." And Charismatic Power: The hypnotic personality that is the trademark of all cult leaders.

John F. Kennedy and Ronald Reagan both had these four powers in great abundance and it made them the most popular presidents in modern history. You can have that kind of power over your buyers if you concentrate on developing those four elements of personal power. When you do, I promise you that you'll see a remarkable transformation in your ability to control your buyers.

So, now you know what gives you personal power over the buyer. In Chapter 36, I'll teach you how to read the personality style of the buyer and adapt your negotiating style to match.

# Chapter 36

# Understanding the Personality of the Buyer

In this chapter, I'll continue with how to handle the players in the negotiating game. In Chapter 35, you learned about personal power, and in this chapter, I'll teach you how to identify the personality style of the buyer and adapt your negotiating style to match. The system I'm going to teach you is based on something that the Ancient Greeks worked out centuries ago, so it is time-tested and proven. However, it may contradict much of the sales training that you have received. I'm sure you've been to one of those training classes that teaches you a canned response to any objection the buyer might raise. Power Sales Negotiators know you've got to adapt what you're doing to the personality styles of the different buyers to whom you sell.

The system is based on two dimensions. The first dimension is the assertiveness level of the buyer. You can tell this by the firmness of the handshake, the directness of his or her responses to your question, and the way the person volunteers his or her name that kind of thing. The assertive buyer wants to get down to business quickly. He or she will shake hands and say, "Come on in and let's see what you have for me." An assertive buyer will quickly make a decision, "I'll take a truckload if you give me a 20-percent discount off list, have them here by the 15th and take care of the freight. Do you want the deal or not?" An unassertive person wants to take time to get to know you. He or she has a long attention span, and so is in the habit of making decisions slowly. This person genuinely needs time to think things over.

Power Sales Negotiators recognize this as a major point of conflict in closing the sale. If you're a fast decision-maker, the less assertive, slow decision-makers drive you up the wall. You'll be thinking, "He's had that proposal for a week now. I call him up and he says he's still thinking about it! For heaven's sake, how long does it take him to make up his mind? It's only $200,000 dollars. It's not that big a deal."

Whereas, if you're an unassertive person you're probably a slow decision-maker yourself, and you're very suspicious of fast decision-makers. You say, "I took the proposal into this buyer and she looked at it briefly, it couldn't have been more than three or four minutes, and said, 'Fine let's go with it.' That company must have the worst credit rating in the world! There's no way we'll ever get paid. It's just not natural for people to make decisions that quickly."

The second dimension is the emotional level of the buyer. This is the same as the left brain versus right brain way of thinking. Emotional, right-brain people are creative and care about people. Unemotional, left-brain people see things in black and white and care about things. Evaluate the way the buyer says things and the warmth with which he or she responds to people to determine his or her emotional personality.

If you combine the assertiveness and emotional dimensions, you come up with four different styles:

First, the assertive-unemotional person whom I call the **Pragmatic**. The Pragmatic buyer will typically have her calls screened. Her secretary will want to know who's calling and what you're calling about before he puts the call through. The business environment will be formal. She'll have a secretary who places her calls and confirms appointments for her and who will usher you into the office (rather than have the buyer come out of her office to meet you). Pragmatics like participation sports such as skiing, scuba diving, flying; she may like golf, but hates how long it takes and typically won't take the time to do it. She's tidy, highly organized, and always dresses formally.

With the Pragmatic, don't waste time with small talk. You're there to make a proposal, not chitchat, and her eyes will glaze over if you try rapport building by talking about the basketball game last night. Don't overload the Pragmatic with information. She'll make a decision with the least amount of information necessary. If you try to sway her with an overly enthusiastic presentation, you'll come across as phony. Expect a fast decision based strictly on facts.

Second is the assertive-emotional person whom I call the **Extrovert**. The Extrovert buyer is friendly and open. He'll place his own telephone calls, doesn't necessarily want his incoming calls screened, will tend to meet you in the lobby if you go to his place of business, and will give you a personal tour of the company. He greets everybody warmly as he walks around the building. He loves the excitement of spectator sports such as baseball or football. He'll probably have pictures of his family in the office. Something a Pragmatic might think is too informal.

Although he likes to spend time talking about his vacation or his hunting trip, if somebody comes into the office for a business decision, or he takes a call while you're there, he'll make the decision quickly.

He's a warm and friendly person, but he's not afraid to say no to you. So, he's personable but at the same time, he's assertive. He's not particularly organized and his desk is probably cluttered. He has poor follow-up, but he's likable and fun to be with.

When you're dealing with an Extrovert, paint an enthusiastic picture of the benefits to him. Get him excited. Talk about his interests. Get to him by telling stories of triumph and disaster. Expect a fast decision based on his level of excitement about the project.

Third is the unassertive-emotional person whom I call the **Amiable**. The Amiable tends to set up barriers. He probably has an unlisted home phone number and may have a "No Peddlers" sign on his front door. He has probably lived in the same home for a long time because he develops relationships with things, as well as with people.

He probably drives an older car because he fears going down to a dealer and getting ground to death by a high-pressure salesperson. Amiables are not entrepreneurs. He prefers managing in a large corporation where the format of the organization protects him from having to make assertive decisions. He seems to have a poor sense of time management. Call him and ask him for an appointment, and he'll tell you to drop by any time. He tends to be disorganized because he can't say no to people. When asked to be on a committee, he has a tough time refusing, so he tends to take on more work than he can handle. His environment is warm and comfortable because he forms a relationship with the things in his life such as homes, furniture, and cars and doesn't like to change them.

When you're dealing with an Amiable, go slowly. Wait until he trusts you. Demonstrate that you really care about people. Be careful, because the slightest little thing will offend this person. Don't high-pressure him because he doesn't like being forced into making a decision. You'll just have to acknowledge that and give him time to think things through. You have to wait until he feels comfortable with you.

The fourth personality style is the unassertive-unemotional person whom I call the **Analytical**. The Analytical would most likely have an engineering or accounting background. She probably has gadget mania and is surrounded by computers, calculators, and phone dialers. She was the first person in her state to have a fax machine at home. She's a very curious person who soaks up information and can't get enough. Show her a book and she'll want to know when and how it was printed.

It's interesting to see an Analytical in a management situation. She feels she can manage everything just by generating massive amounts of information. Analyticals are very precise about punctuality, so you'll never hear her saying, "I'll be there around lunch time."

She would say, "I'll be there at twelve-fifteen." She's also very precise about figures so she won't tell you that something cost just over a hundred dollars. She'll tell you it cost $114.16. She loves precision, so when you tell her the specifications of your product, carry it out to two decimal places.

With the Analytical, be accurate. Ask her what day of the week it is, and she'll tell you, "It's Wednesday. Except on the Island of Tonga, where it's already Thursday morning." She's fascinated by analysis and has charts and graphs for everything. So, when she asks you for figures, give them to the penny. Be prepared to give every little detail of the operation. Try to build rapport by talking about her interests, which probably include engineering and computer technology.

Once you realize how easy it is to identify the personality style of the buyer, you'll find yourself questioning many of the things you have been taught in sales training.

For example, you were taught to always be enthusiastic, weren't you? How can you expect the buyer to be enthusiastic about your product or service if you're not? Well, enthusiasm is wonderful with the Extrovert because that kind of person feeds off of excitement.

And it's great with the Amiable, because he gets a warm feeling from the enthusiasm. "You can just sense how good he feels about that, so it must be a good idea."

But the Pragmatic is turned off by enthusiasm. "Oh, don't give me that phony sales pitch," she's thinking. "Just give me the facts I need to make a decision."

And there's no way you can tell me that an Analytical will be bowled over by enthusiasm. She's not going to make a decision until she feels that she has enough information.

Another thing that I'm sure you learned in sales training is to dominate the conversation. When the buyer asks you a question, answer with a question.

"Can you deliver in 30 days for me?"

"Would you like it delivered in 30 days?"

"Does it come in blue?"

"Would you like it in blue?"

"Can you give me 90 days to pay?"

"Would you like 90 days to pay?" And so on.

Well, this is great with the Analytical because she loves questions. She'll sit there all day asking and answering questions.

And it's great with the Amiable because it's a sign that you care about him.

But when a Pragmatic asks you a question, she wants answers. She doesn't want to play verbal Ping-Pong with you.

It's the same with the assertive Extrovert. He won't warm to you unless you deal with him in a straightforward and open manner. He'll make a fast decision but it will be based on facts.

Another thing that you've probably been taught is that people buy with emotion, not logic, and the only reason they need any logic at all is to justify the emotional decision they just made.

Well that's true with the Extrovert personality. Donald Trump spent millions on pink Italian marble for the lobby of Trump Tower because it felt like the right thing to do.

It's true with the Amiable because the emotion translates into a warm feeling about you and what you do.

But Pragmatics don't spend money with emotion; they spend because it's going to generate the return they want.

Analyticals don't make a buying decision with emotion either. They'll make a buying decision when they feel that all the numbers are in line.

Recognize that you will have the most difficulty with the personality style that is different from you on both the assertive and emotional dimensions. If you are an assertive-unemotional Pragmatic, you love other Pragmatics. They are down-to-earth, no-nonsense people and if you ask them a question, you'll get an answer. When you want a decision, you'll get it and they'll live with it. It's when you have to deal with the unassertive-emotional Amiable, that you run into difficulty. You're thinking quickly, unemotionally, but they're thinking slowly and emotionally.

You'll make a proposal to an Amiable and not see a reason in the world why he shouldn't go along with it. To you it's clear that you can provide a better product at a lower price than his present vendor can. So, he ought to dump that other vendor and go with you, but he holds back. He's thinking, "I don't feel comfortable with you yet. I want to do business with people I feel comfortable with. Don't tell me how much you know until you tell me how much you care."

Conversely, the Amiable will have the most difficulty with Pragmatics such as you. You seem so hardheaded and impersonal to this kind of person. You seem to be all business with no feeling for people. So, the Amiable doesn't feel good about doing business with you.

If you're an assertive-emotional Extrovert, you love other Extroverts. They're fun people who will go off and do exciting things at the drop of a hat. It's when you have to deal with the unassertive-unemotional Analytical that you run into difficulties. To you, Analyticals always seem to need too much information. They're too much into the details and don't seem able to see the big picture. To you, they're far too cautious in the way they do things because accuracy is next to Godliness to an Analytical.

When an Analytical says, "When will you deliver the shipment?"

He wants to hear you say, "January 16th by 3:15 in the afternoon."

He doesn't want to hear, "Oh, about the middle of January or so." He wants to hear it out to the minute.

When he says, "What's the thickness of the paint you'll use on the casing," he doesn't want to hear, "Oh, about medium I guess." He wants to hear it down to a thousandth of an inch.

Conversely, the Analytical, thinks that you as an Extrovert are too flippant. You're too easy-going, and you go off on different tangents without really knowing all the information that you ought to know about the situation.

## Differences of Personality Styles

Now let's talk about how each of these personality styles negotiate differently.

The Pragmatic in a negotiation situation turns into a Street Fighter. A Street Fighter is a person whose only goal in the negotiation is to win, and to her winning means that somebody else has to lose, and what's wrong with that? "That's the way the world is—don't waste my time with all this wishy-washy win-win nonsense. Why on earth would I be concerned about their needs in the negotiations? That's what they're here for, and I expect them to fight as hard for what they want, as I'm going to fight for what I want."

You would think that the Street Fighter would be the one you'd least like to see sitting behind a buyer's desk, but they have a vulnerable flaw. Their flaw is that they become obsessed with one issue in the negotiation because they see negotiating as a game to be won or lost and they must have a way to score the game. So, the Street Fighter buyer may decide that winning the negotiation with you means that he gets you down to a lower price than her present supplier. So, she will become obsessed with that one issue. If you realize this, you'll find that she will give away everything else in order to attain that goal. Let's say that you sell commercial real estate and you have a Street Fighter seller who has made up his mind that he won't take a penny less than $10 million for his shopping center. If you take him an offer at $9.8 million, he will turn it down because he would feel that he was losing. However, if you took him an offer at $10 million that asked him to carry back a $1 million dollar straight note with 6 percent interest added, due and payable in 10 years, he would accept it. It is a worse offer than the $9.8 million cash-out offer, if you consider the time value of money, but he will turn that down because it doesn't meet the criteria by which he's scoring the game.

Another thing about the Street Fighter is that in order for him to feel that he won, he must see that someone else is losing. Don't talk win-win to a Street Fighter. Instead, bleed over him and tell him how much you're hurting.

The Extrovert turns into a Den Mother as a negotiator. A Den Mother is someone who gets so excited about things that they tend to lose perspective. This is the salesperson who is organizing a softball team and he's so excited and enthusiastic about it! It doesn't occur to him that there's nobody in the entire world who wants to play softball on Tuesday night.

Den Mothers are the people most likely to have the whole negotiations fall down around them and not realize there was a problem. You'll see them come back into their office and kick the desk. "They went with the other supplier! How can they do this to me? I was out drinking with them until midnight the other night."

The Amiable tends to turn into a Pacifier as a negotiator. The Pacifier's objective in the negotiations is not so much to win, as to see that everybody is happy. It's interesting to see the opposite personality style, the Street Fighter, negotiating with the Pacifier. The Street Fighter will grind every last dime out of negotiations, convinced there's not another penny left on the table, and when it's all over the Pacifier will turn to the Street Fighter and say, "Now are you sure this is fair? I wouldn't want to take advantage of you."

The Analytical tends to turn into an Executive style negotiator. Typically the Analytical buyer was schooled as an engineer or an accountant, so everything's been okay as long as it's been buttoned down, nailed down, and in its place. They don't like the push and the shove of negotiating. They like everything to be rigid and in place, and their favorite expression is, "It's the principle of the thing."

The opposite personality style, the Extrovert/Den Mother will say, "Hey look! We're only talking five hundred bucks here, so for heavens sakes let's split the difference and get the thing going."

And the Analytical/Executive style negotiator will say, "Well I understand we're talking $500. Actually, because you're proposing that we split it, we're talking only $250 aren't we? But at this point, it's the principle of the thing I'm concerned about."

So, if you're an Analytical, be careful that you're not too rigid in the way you negotiate.

Now let's take a look at these different personality styles and see how their style of negotiating is different from what I want you to become, which is a Win-Win Power Negotiator. Let's look at each element of the negotiations.

## Goals in negotiations

The Pragmatic/Street Fighter's goal is clear. Her goal is victory—this person plans to win in the negotiations.

The Extrovert/Den Mother's goal is to influence the other people. He has so much fun changing other peoples' minds that he loves to take a position against the other side, just to see if he can turn their thinking around.

The Amiable/Pacifier's goal is agreement. He feels that if he can get everybody to agree on something everything else will fall into place.

The Analytical/Executive's goal is to have order in the negotiations. She wants to get the negotiation on a formal format so that the procedures established produce a solution.

But the goal of the Win-Win Power Negotiator, which is what I want you to become, is a wise outcome for all parties involved.

## Relationships in negotiation

The Street Fighter has a tendency to frighten people. He's sitting there on the edge of hostility and he's implying, "If you don't go along with what I want, it's going to get very, very uncomfortable here, and you're not going to like it."

The Den Mother personality, tries to do it all by inspiring the other person. Getting that person so excited that she'll be able to sway them over.

The Pacifier wants to develop relationships. His philosophy is: "If we like each other well enough, we'll all agree."

And the Executive really ignores the relationships and negotiates strictly based on facts.

The Win-Win Power Negotiator learns how to separate people from the problem. This is done by bringing the people back from their emotional relationships with each other and concentrating on the resolution of the issue.

## Negotiating styles of the four personality styles

The style of the Street Fighter is very hard and domineering.

The style of the Den Mother is excitable.

The style of the Pacifier is soft (maybe too soft).

The style of the Executive is remaining detached from the personalities.

The Win-Win Power Negotiator leans how to be soft on the people, but hard on the problem. He's easy going, friendly, likable, and courteous with all the people involved in the negotiations, but he keeps hammering away and concentrates on the problems.

## Personality style faults as negotiators

The Street Fighter, the dominant personality, tends to dig into a particular position. Determined to get what she wants from the negotiation, she won't budge even when it would be better to yield.

The Den Mother tends to ignore the others and is not sensitive enough to realize what's really going on in the negotiations.

The Pacifier is too easily swayed.

The Executive is inflexible.

## Different methods of negotiating

The Street Fighter demands losses from the other people. He doesn't feel that he can win unless other people lose.

The Den Mother wants to inspire people, to get them turned on to a particular idea. She believes that if people are excited about it enough, they'll go for it.

The Pacifier tends to accept losses. His theory is that if he make concessions, the other side will want to reciprocate.

The Executive is too rigid in her style of negotiating.

The Win-Win Power Negotiator learns how to create options in the negotiations where nobody loses.

So, a critical issue in the negotiating process is that the Win-Win Power Negotiator works to get people off the positions that they have taken, largely because of their personality styles, so that they can concentrate on interests. This is a key point because positions can be 180 degrees apart, whereas interests can be identical.

Examine the changing relationship between the United States and Russia. For 40 years the Russians had adopted a position that "there's no sense arguing with the capitalists; they're not going to change until they dominate the world. Why negotiate with them?" Similarly, we Americans had taken the position that the Russians were so inflexible that it was a waste of time to talk to them. We'd known that ever since Khrushchev pounded his shoe on the table at the United Nations. That they wouldn't stop until they dominated the world with their philosophy. We took an equally tough position. We were calling them an Evil Empire.

Those were positions that both sides have taken. For 40 years, we concentrated on positions. Without question, we both have a mutual interest in world peace. We both have an interest in reducing our military expenditures. We both have an interest in becoming trading partners. They had all that titanium. We needed it for our golf clubs, but we couldn't see that while we were focused on our positions!

So, a Power Sales Negotiator learns to get people off positions that they have taken, so that they can concentrate on their mutual interests. The key to being able to do this is to become familiar with the different personality styles of your buyers and learn how they approach things differently. Then, although they may have taken a radically different position from yours, work on getting them off that position and concentrating on your mutual interests.

# Chapter 37

# Win-Win Sales Negotiating

To complete this course in Power Sales Negotiating let's talk more about win-win negotiating. Instead of trying to dominate buyers and trick them into doing things they wouldn't normally do, I believe that you should work with buyers to work out your problems and develop a solution with which both of you can win. Your reaction to that may be, "Roger, you obviously don't know much about the kind of selling that I do. I live in a dog-eat-dog world. My buyers don't take any prisoners. They eat their young. There's no such thing as win-win in my industry. When I'm selling I'm obviously trying to get the highest price I possibly can, and the buyer is obviously trying to get the lowest possible price. How on earth can we both win in the negotiation?"

So, let's start out with the most important issue: What do we mean when we say win-win? Does it really mean that both sides win? Or does it mean that both sides lose equally so that it's fair? What if each side thinks that he or she has won and that the other side lost—would that be win-win?

Before you dismiss that possibility, think about it more. What if you leave with a big order and you're thinking, "I won! I would have dropped the price even more if the buyer had been a better negotiator"? However, the buyer is thinking that she won and that she would have paid more if you had been a better negotiator. So, both of you think that you won and the other person lost. Is that win-win? Yes, I believe it is, as long as it's a permanent feeling. As long as neither of you wakes up tomorrow morning thinking, "Son of a gun, now I know what he did to me. Wait until I see him again."

That's why I stress doing the things that service the perception that the other side won, such as not jumping at the first offer, asking for more than you expect to get, flinching, positioning for easy acceptance, and so on.

Besides constantly servicing the perceptions that the other side won, there are three fundamental rules to observe.

## Rule 1: Don't narrow the negotiation down to just one issue

If you resolve all the other issues and the only thing left to negotiate is price, somebody does have to win, and somebody does have to lose. As long as you keep more than one issue on the table, you can always work trade-offs so that the buyer doesn't mind conceding on price because you're able to offer something in return.

Sometimes buyers try to treat your product as a commodity by saying, "We buy this stuff by the ton. As long as it meets specs, we don't mind who made it or where it comes from." They are trying to treat this as a one-issue negotiation to persuade you that the only way you can make a meaningful concession is to lower your price. When that's the case you should do everything possible to put other issues, such as delivery, terms, packaging, and guarantee onto the table so that you can use these items for trade-offs and get away from the perception that this is a one-issue negotiation.

At a seminar, a commercial real estate salesperson came up to me. He was excited because he'd almost completed "negotiating a contract for more than a year," he told me. "And we've almost got it resolved. In fact, we've resolved everything except price and we're only $72,000 apart." I flinched because I knew that now, because he'd narrowed it down to one issue, there had to be a winner and there had to be a loser. However close they may be, they were heading for trouble.

Fortunately, there are always many elements that are important in negotiations, other than the main issue. So, the art of win-win negotiating requires that you piece together those elements like a jigsaw puzzle so that both people can win.

Rule one is: Don't narrow the negotiations down to just one issue. Although we may resolve impasses by finding a common ground on small issues to keep the negotiation moving, as I taught you in Chapter 33, you should never narrow it down to one issue.

## Rule 2: Understand that people are not out for the same thing

We all have an overriding tendency to assume that other people want what we want—that what's important to us will be important to them, but that's not true.

The biggest trap into which salespeople fall is assuming that price is the dominant issue in a negotiation. Obviously, many other elements are important to the buyer. You must convince him of the quality of your product or service. He needs to know that you will deliver on time. He wants to know that you will give adequate management supervision to his account. Explain how flexible you are on payment terms. Does your company have the financial strength to be a partner of theirs? Do you have the support of a well-trained and motivated work force? These all come into play, as well as half-a-dozen other factors. When you have satisfied the buyer that you can meet all those requirements then, and only then, does price become a deciding factor.

The second key to win-win negotiating is: Don't assume that they want what you want. Because if you do, you further make the assumption that anything you do in the negotiations to help them get what they want takes you further away from what you want.

Win-win negotiating can only come when you understand that people don't want the same things in the negotiation. Good Power Sales Negotiating becomes not just a matter of getting what you want, but also being concerned about the other person getting what he or she wants. One of the most powerful thoughts you can have when you're negotiating with a buyer is not, "What can I get from them?" but "What can I give them that won't take away from my position?" Because people will give you what you want in a negotiation when you give them what they want.

## Rule 3: Don't be too greedy

Don't try to get the last dollar off the table. You may feel that you triumphed, but does that help you if the buyer felt that you vanquished him? That last dollar left on the table is a very expensive dollar to pick up. So, don't try to get it all, but leave something on the table so that the buyer feels that he or she won also.

# Rule 4: Put something back on the table

Do something extra, over and above what you promised to do. Give your buyers a little extra service. Care about them a little more than you have to. Then you'll find that the little extra that they didn't have to negotiate for means more to them than everything for which they did have to negotiate.

# Key points to remember

➤ Don't narrow the negotiation down to just one issue.

➤ Don't assume that helping the buyer get what he wants takes away from your position. You're not out for the same thing. Poor negotiators try to force the buyer to get off the positions that they've taken. Power Sales Negotiators know that even when positions are 180 degrees apart, the interests of both sides can be neutral, so they work to get people off their positions and concentrate on their interests.

➤ Don't be greedy. Don't try to get the last dollar off the table.

➤ Put something back on the table. Do more than they bargained for.

# Postscript

Let me leave you with one thought. If you understand the power of this simple thought and make it the cornerstone of your career, it will make everything else in your career drop into place. Here's my advice to you: Forget everything else you're doing and concentrate on getting better at what you do.

Quit worrying about how you're going to get your boss to give you that raise in pay and concentrate on getting better at what you do.

Stop fretting about how you're going to get that promotion to sales manager or how you're going to get assigned to that larger territory and concentrate on getting better at what you do.

Forget your anxiety about how you're going to pay next month's bills and concentrate on getting better at what you do.

How can you get better at what you do? Concentrate on how to get that order without having to discount your price. Focus on how to get your buyers to give you all of their business instead of just part of it. Intensify your efforts to have the buyers trust you so much that they're asking for your advice on what to do. Just get better at what you do, and when that becomes your focus, everything else will fall into place for you. The money to pay those bills will find you; your sales manager will be begging you to take over that prize territory, and your boss will be pleading with you to take that promotion. When getting better at what you do becomes your obsession, everything else drops into place.

Good luck in all your negotiations and remember: Nothing happens until somebody sells something—at a profit!

# About the Author

Roger Dawson was born in England and immigrated to California in 1962. He became a United States citizen 10 years later. Formerly the president of one of California's largest real estate companies, he became a full-time author and professional speaker in 1982.

Roger Dawson is the founder of The Power Negotiating Institute, a California based organization. His Nightingale-Conant cassette program *Secrets of Power Negotiating* is the largest-selling business cassette program ever published. Several of his books have been main selections of major book clubs.

Companies and associations throughout North America call on Dawson for his expertise in negotiation, persuasion, and decision-making, and for motivational keynote speeches. His seminar company, Roger Dawson Productions, conducts seminars throughout the country on Power Negotiating, Power Sales Negotiating, Power Persuasion, Confident Decision-Making, and High Achievement.

Roger Dawson Productions
P.O. Box 2040
La Habra, California 90631
Telephone: 800 YDAWSON [932-9766]

# Also by Roger Dawson

## Books
*You Can Get Anything You Want*
*Secrets of Power Negotiating*
*Secrets of Power Persuasion*
*The Confident Decision Maker*
*The 13 Secrets of Power Performance*
*Secrets of Power Negotiating for Salespeople*
*Secrets of Power Persuasion for Salespeople*
*Secrets of Power Problem Solving*

### (with Mike Summey)
*The Weekend Millionaires Guide to Real Estate Investing*
*Weekend Millionaire Mindset*
*Weekend Millionaire FAQ*
*Weekend Millionaire Secrets to Negotiating Real Estate*

## Audio Programs
*Secrets of Power Negotiating*
*Secrets of Power Persuasion*
*Secrets of Power Performance*
*Confident Decision Making*
*The Personality of Achievers*
*Power Negotiating for Salespeople*

## Video Training Programs
*Guide to Everyday Negotiating*
*Guide to Business Negotiating*
*Guide to Advanced Negotiating Power*
*Power Negotiating for Salespeople* (a 12-part series)

## Speeches and Seminars

If you hire speakers for your company, or influence the selection of speakers at your association, you should learn more about Roger Dawson's speeches and seminars. He will customize his presentation to your company or industry so that you get a unique presentation tailored to your needs. You can also arrange to audio or videotape the presentation for use as a continuous training resource.

## Roger Dawson's Presentations Include:

*Secrets of Power Negotiating*
*Secrets of Power Persuasion*
*Confident Decision Making*
*The 13 Secrets of Power Performance*

To get more information and receive a complimentary press kit, please call, write, e-mail, or fax:

The Power Negotiating Institute
1045 East Road
La Habra Heights, CA 90631 USA

Phone:    800–YDAWSON (932–9766)
Fax:    562–697–1397
E-mail:    *Dawsonprod@aol.com*
Website:    *www.RogerDawson.com*

# Audio CD and Video Programs

Following is a listing of Roger Dawson's audio and video programs that you can order from the following:

The Power Negotiating Institute

1045 East Road

La Habra Heights, CA 90631 USA

Phone:     800–YDAWSON (932–9766)

Fax:        562–697–1397

E-mail:    *Dawsonprod@aol.com*

Website:   *www.RogerDawson.com*

## Audio CD Programs

Secrets of Power Negotiating                                   $69.95

Six hours of great training on 6 audio CDs. This is one of the largest-selling business audio programs ever published, with sales of more than $38 million. You'll learn 20 negotiating gambits that are sure-fire winners. Going beyond the mere mechanics of the power negotiating process, Roger Dawson helps you learn what influences people, and how to recognize and adjust to different negotiating styles, so you can get what you want, regardless of the situation.

Also, you'll learn:

›   A new way of pressuring people without confrontation.

›   The one unconscious decision you must never make in a negotiation.

›   The five standards by which every negotiation should be judged.

›   Why saying yes too soon is always a mistake.

›   How to gather the information you need without the other side knowing.

›   The three stages terrorist negotiators use to defuse crisis situations, and much, much more.

## Power Negotiating for Salespeople $69.95

Six hours of great training on 6 audio CDs. This program that supplements and enhances Roger Dawson's famous generic negotiating program *Secrets of Power Negotiating,* teaches salespeople how to negotiate with buyers and get higher prices without having to give away extras, such as freight and extended payment terms. It's the most in-depth program ever created for selling at higher prices than your competition and still maintaining long-term relationships with your customers. It's guaranteed to dramatically improve your profit margins, or we'll give your money back.

> **Special Offer**. Invest in both *Secrets of Power Negotiating* and *Power Negotiating for Salespeople* and save $30.
> Both for only $110.

## Secrets of Power Persuasion $69.95

Six hours of great training on 6 audio CDs. In this program, Roger Dawson shows you the strategies and tactics that will enable you to persuade people in virtually any situation. Not by using threats or phony promises, but because they perceive that it's in their best interest to do what you say.

You'll learn:

› Why credibility and above all, consistency are the cornerstones of getting what you want.

› You'll learn verbal persuasion techniques that defuse resistance and demonstrate the validity of your thinking.

› To develop an overwhelming aura of personal *charisma* that will naturally cause people to like you, respect you, and gladly agree with you.

› It's just a matter of mastering the specific, practical behavioral techniques that Roger Dawson presents in a highly entertaining manner.

## Secrets of Power Performance $69.95

Six hours of great training on 6 audio CDs. With this program, you'll learn how to get the best from yourself and those around you! Roger Dawson believes that we are all capable of doing more than we think we're capable of. Isn't that true for you? Aren't you doing far more now than you thought you could do five years ago? With the life-changing secrets revealed in this best selling program, you'll be able to transform your world in the next five years!

## Also by Roger Dawson

Confident Decision Making                                    $69.95

Six hours of great training on 6 audio CDs. Decisions are the building blocks of your life. The decisions you've made have given you everything you now have. The decisions you'll make from this point on will be responsible for everything that happens to you for the rest of your life. Wouldn't it be wonderful to know that, from this point on, you'll always be making the right choice? All you have to do is listen to this landmark program.

You'll learn:

‣ How to quickly and accurately categorize your decision.

‣ How to expand your options with a 10-step creative thinking process.

‣ How to find the right answer with reaction tables and decision trees.

‣ How to harness the power of synergism with the principle of huddling.

‣ How to know exactly what and how your boss, customer, or employee will decide, and dozens more powerful techniques.

## Video Training Programs

Guide to Business Negotiating          One hour DVD video  $55
Guide to Everyday Negotiating          One hour DVD video  $55
Guide to Advanced Negotiating Power    One hour DVD video  $55

If you're in any way responsible for training or supervising other people, these videos will liven up your staff meetings and turn your people into master negotiators. Your sales and profits will soar as you build new win-win relationships with your customers. Then use these programs to develop a training library for your employees' review, and for training new hires.

Power Negotiating for Salespeople          12-PART VIDEO SERIES  $499

Think how your sales and your profit margins would soar, if you could have Roger Dawson speak at your sales meetings once a month! Now you can, with this new series of twelve 30-minute videotapes designed just for this purpose. Dawson goes one-on-one with your salespeople to show them how to out-negotiate your buyers. Play one a month at your sales meetings and watch your people become masterful negotiators!

# Index